Initiation to Adulthood

Initiation to Adulthood

An Ancient Rite of Passage
in Contemporary Form

William O. Roberts, Jr.

THE PILGRIM PRESS
New York

All scripture quotations, unless otherwise indicated, are from the Revised Standard Version of the Bible, © 1946, 1952, 1971, 1973 by the Division of Christian Education of the National Council of the Churches of Christ in the United States of America.

Scripture quotations indicated by NEB are from the *New English Bible.* © The Delegates of the Oxford University Press and the Syndics of the Cambridge University Press 1961, 1970. Reprinted by permission.

Scripture quotations indicated by K have been translated by Aidan Kavanagh.

Quotations from The Apostolic Tradition are from Grove Liturgical Study, No. 8, *Hippolytus: A Text for Students,* translated and edited by Geoffrey J. Cuming, copyright 1976 by Geoffrey S. Cuming. Reprinted by permission of the publisher, Grove Books, Bramcote, Nottingham, Great Britain.

Library of Congress Cataloging in Publication Data

Roberts, William O., 1942-
    Initiation to adulthood.

    1. Initiation rites—Religious aspects—Christianity.
I. Title.
BV873.I54R63   1982   265'.2   82-18544
ISBN 0-8298-0629-6

Cover Design: Gloria Claudia Ortiz

Illustrations for Parts One and Two: Judith Jerome

The Pilgrim Press, 132 West 31 Street, New York, New York 10001

To Melissa

Contents

PART TWO

Initiation to Adulthood

Prologue

Our culture is missing something. Something important. We have lost one of our rites. The time has come to rediscover it.

The rite we have lost is generally called Initiation: the Rite of Passage to Adulthood. It was one of several rites that marked and enabled the passage from one stage of existence to another: from non-being to being at birth, from being two separate persons to becoming one flesh at marriage, from being alive to being dead at the time of death. All these passages have rites to express and define them. For birth there is the baptism. For marriage there is the wedding. For death there is the funeral. But for the passage to adulthood there is nothing, or next to nothing, in our culture. Norman O. Brown, the philosopher of history, describes our situation very simply. "Religious remnants of such practices still exist; but they have now shrunk to historical isolated relics out of step with the schedules of status change in all other areas of modern life."[1]

Through its many denominations and traditions, the Christian church exercises major responsibility for preserving and renewing not only our faith but also the rituals that express our faith. The church needs to be aware of the disservice done to society through its failure to initiate youth into the adult world. In the vacuum, untold adolescents discover that they must initiate themselves into adulthood, very often through experimentation with alcohol, drugs, sex, or violence. The results of this self-initiation are reported daily in our newspapers: soaring statistics on teenage pregnancies, automobile and motorcycle accidents, adoles-

3

cent suicides, high school violence, drug and alcohol abuse. Those persons who counsel or parent young people know still more: the endless waiting lists for adolescent units at our mental hospitals, the anguish within families, the confusion and pain of the adolescents themselves. Joseph Campbell in his classic on the significance of myth and ritual writes:

> There can be no question, the psychological dangers through which earlier generations were guided by the symbols and spiritual exercises of the mythological and religious inheritance, we must face alone, or at best, with only tentative, impromptu, and not too often very effective guidance. [This is our problem as modern] enlightened individuals, for whom all the gods and devils have been rationalized out of existence.[2]

Several years ago the people at First Church in Middletown, Connecticut, and I became aware that something was missing in our ministry. In a fascinating, creative process, we set about the task of forming an old-new rite of passage to adulthood.

The awareness began with an ache. At first it was merely the dull pain that comes from knowing something is not as it should be. As time went on we began to locate the part of the body that was causing our distress. Our young people, who had a social experience in a youth group and a learning experience in the church school and confirmation class, began to express their unhappiness with what was being offered. Like most sensitive beings, the church responded to their pain by trying to alleviate it. Our attention was soon drawn to the confirmation program, as we tried over and again to "firm up" confirmation.

First we read the new confirmation materials from several denominations, each of which was trying to do something new. But they all seemed lacking. Next we moved to the secular world. We talked with some of the most creative teachers in the school system. They showed us how to give confirmands more freedom through individualized instruc-

4

tional packages, and then helped us to create our own new thing, a self-guided means to confirmation. But in spite of all our hard work and good intentions, this didn't catch on either. Our adolescents didn't want more freedom. We didn't know what they wanted. Or what they needed.

Then, as is the option of a senior minister in a multiple staff church, *we* solved *our* problem by transferring it to someone else. The Associate Minister, fresh out of seminary with all the latest thinking on the matter of confirmation, was assigned responsibility for the next confirmation class. As it turned out, he could accomplish all other tasks in the church with great success, but not the confirmation class. And so *his* problem became *ours* again.

By now the ache had begun to ripen with the prodding of the young people, who, in good faith, would not submit to another feeble attempt to prepare them for the act of confirming their faith. One night the group went to see a motion picture called "The Trial of Billie Jack," in which they saw for the first time an initiation rite. One of the young women—an exceptionally responsible, caring and honest person, who was secure enough to affirm herself by saying "no" to confirmation—came to me as soon as she could and presented me with the good-bad news of their discovery.

"Bill," she said, "what we saw in that movie was the real thing. What we have in this church is not 'the real thing.'"

With that the ache became unbearable. I clearly was ready for a vision that would give form to a new being. The vision came with a suddenness and a power that was both frightening and exciting. It came at the end of eight days of silence during which I was disciplined by the spiritual exercises of Ignatius Loyola.

A few days later, back in the pulpit of First Church, I shared the vision with the congregation in a sermon. The occasion was Pentecost, 1974. The text for the sermon was Joel 2:28:

I will pour out my spirit on all flesh;
　your sons and your daughters shall prophesy,
　　your old men shall dream dreams,
　　and your young men shall see visions.

The celebration reflected the fact that the passages of birth, marriage and death were already part of the congregation's life: recently we had shared a baptism, a wedding, and a funeral. But on that occasion, we finally admitted to one another that we had lost one of our rites. Only the rite of passage to adulthood was absent. And we promised to dedicate ourselves to rediscover it.

The sermon ended with confirmation. It began with these words.

I have had a vision
　a beautiful vision that I wish to share with you before I leave you.
It is a vision of a People of God
　who gather together in a great old church building just off Main Street in a city that rests on a river.

The church has at its center a big room, shaped like a disc or saucer. And it's carpeted and comfortable and warm.
And the walls of the church are created of a most amazing substance—they are strong, able to support this gigantic roof—like a big dome. But they are invisible, and porous. And you can walk right through them, so you can come from the world into the church or go from the church into the world without feeling the change—and you can get in or out anywhere in the room—and you can hear what's going on inside if you're outside and what's going on outside if you're inside.
And the wind can blow right through those walls.
So the air is always fresh.

6

Sometimes it's gusting, sometimes it's calm
  but always it moves back
  and forth as it will.

And in the center of this room
  there is a bowl,
  and the river that flows
  under the city and the church
  happens to have a spring, an eternal
  spring, that bubbles up right under
  the church and causes waters, living
  waters, to keep flowing in and out of
  the bowl.

And in this room there are people
  People of God
  who look like all the rest
  of God's people
  but who are a
  bit different
  because they
  call *themselves the*
  People of God.
The People are milling about.
At first glance I didn't see any order or system to their
  milling about. They were just talking—quietly or not so
  quietly.
As I watched I began to realize that there was some
  meaning to that milling around . . . that every now and
  then some person or persons came up near the bowl
  and talked to one another and to a person who seemed
  always to be standing near the bowl.
  I listened in.
A man said to a woman
  "I do."
And she said to him
  "And I do."

And he said,
*   "I, Keith, take you, Barbara, to be my wife."*
And there was a powerful feeling in the air.

And then I saw another group next to the bowl.
*   And they had a baby and the baby looked with wide*
*   eyes, filled with wonder and awe . . . and seemed to see*
*   things that the older folks missed.*
*   And the parents said*
*   "We do."*
*   And the people near by said*
*   "We do."*
And the person who seemed always to be standing near
*   the bowl touched the water and the child and said*
*   "Angela Lee, I baptize you in the name of the Father,*
*   and of . . . . "*
and there was a powerful feeling in the air.

And next I discovered another group that had come to the
*   old building with a special purpose. They had come to*
*   reminisce about a friend who had died. And as I*
*   listened in, somehow, the dear old woman seemed to be*
*   particularly alive, which was strange, because the hard*
*   and painful yet joyful fact was that she had lived a full*
*   life of 83 years and now she was dead. And I thought*
*   . . . the air in that room sure is powerful; why, it seems*
*   to give life to the dead.*

And then I noticed a most interesting group off in one
*   corner. They were teenagers—sitting and talking—and*
*   I listened.*
*   "What does it mean to be a church member?"*
*   Silence.*
*   "Well, what does it mean 'to come of age'?"*
*   Silence.*
*   "Well, what other ceremonies do we have that help us*
*   to acknowledge that we are adults?"*
*   Silence.*

8

And then
 —we get drivers' licenses,
 —we can vote,
 —we become "a woman,"
 —we graduate from high school.
 We get big enough, old enough,
 smart enough,
 person enough
 to go and drink out of the bowl ourselves.
One who stood by the bowl said, "And that is not to be taken lightly. You know, in other societies and in other times this was a deadly serious event."

"I know," said one. "I heard about an Indian tribe that took its young people—especially young men, and sent them out to the woods, well, more like a desert . . . no, it was a vision pit. And there they stayed for four days, fasted, fought snakes, until they had a vision that helped them to know what they were to do with their lives."

"And I know", said another, "of the Jewish custom of Bar Mitzvah, which means 'son of the command,' and where it is believed that the person Bar Mitzvahed is now mature enough to make his own decisions about God's will for his life . . . and as proof of that . . . to read TORAH scripture . . . to the whole congregation."

"And I know," said the person who had been standing near the bowl, "I now know that in the Christian church we too should have a rite that helps all persons to find their own vision of what they want in life, that helps all persons to come to their own understanding of God's command. And if you'll come with me way into the future and deep into the past, we'll find that rite; we'll find that rite."

*It was obvious from the looks on the faces of the young people
that not all of this seemed real. And yet,*

    *in that vision there seemed to be a willingness to trust the
future and to trust the spirit. And the young people slowly
but surely began to move closer and closer to the bowl, to
look into it, to hear about it, even to dip into it to get some of
the living water.*

*And again there was a powerful feeling in the air. And
suddenly a realization came out of the vision.*

    I came to know in new and important ways . . . life moves.
      *moves from non-being to being through birth,
      moves from being a child to being an adult,
      moves from being two persons to being one person,
      moves from being alive to being dead.*

*Yet, with all that movement, life is also grounded and centered,
grounded in God and centered in Christ.*

And even more,

    *it is empowered by the Holy Spirit . . . and I thought again
of the air in that old church building off Main Street in the
city that rests on a river . . . the air that blew in and out and
through those wonderful porous walls.*

And I realized

    *that air was the very breath of God blowing where it would
and filling all of us with the Spirit . . . and I heard again that
ancient promise that someday we would be so filled with the
Spirit . . . that we would be nothing but the Breath of the
Spirit blowing in us.*

Once the vision was delivered to God's people, the ache
eased a bit, but the call implicit in the vision could not simply
be delivered in a sermon. It had to be embodied in a living
thing—a brand new thing that was also a very old thing.

The third step in the creative process—if you accept the
ache and the vision as the first two steps—was researching in
the areas of anthropology and psychology. These two
disciplines provided us with the shape of the initiation and
with much of its content.

The fourth step was the implementation of the vision. In the fall of 1974 a group of approximately twenty young people in the eighth and ninth grades became "the Initiation Group," convenanting with one another to embark upon a two-year journey leading them to adulthood. Two years later another group of young people formed the second Initiation Group. In addition, the congregation established two other youth groups, one on either side of the Initiation Group: a Pre-Initiation Group for those who were younger, and a Graduate group for those who had passed through their initiation. In 1978 and 1980 the third and fourth Initiation Groups were formed. By 1982, nearly one hundred adolescents had been initiated.

The content of the initiation experiences was determined to a great extent by the initiates. Without knowing it, they have raised the issues of their lives and asked their questions. We who have taken responsibility for their growth have tried to structure experiences and impart knowledge to help them deal with their own issues and answer their own questions.

In the course of living out the early initiations, there was one area of concern that had gone untended. The concern was first expressed by a Deaconess at the conclusion of the first two-year initiation. As we were preparing for the final ritual—the baptism, confirmation, new communion—she asked me to explain just how all this was a rite of the Christian church. At that time I could only answer with a plea. "Trust me," I said. "I just know it's the right thing to do." But within me there was a legion of anxieties that grew out of her question.

Five years ago, my first attempt to answer that question proved futile. I must have looked in the wrong places, talked to the wrong people, or read the wrong books. Everywhere I turned I heard the same answer, perhaps most simply stated by a denominational executive: "In Christianity we confirm faith. We don't initiate people."

Unwilling to give up the vision, I went back to the

scriptures themselves and found initiation motifs everywhere. Emboldened by my findings, I once again set out to answer the question, "How is initiation to adulthood a rite of the Christian church?" This time, guided by the suggestions of people who had seen our initiation and come to share the vision, I looked in different places, talked to different people, and read different books. Lo and behold, I had an experience like walking into a surprise party. The room was filled with people who had arrived here before me. As I talked to various people, I had the sure sense that, even though we had come by different routes, we had arrived at the same place. What they had discovered through careful research and scholarly dialogue, our church had found by following the vision and playing our hunch. We all knew that initiation to adulthood was a lost rite. We could rejoice and be exceeding glad that it was being rediscovered and returned to its rightful place in the life of the Christian church and the lives of Christian adolescents.

This book is my attempt to share what we have found and how we have tried to return the rite of initiation to adulthood to its rightful place in the life of the church.

The book has two separate but related parts. Part One presents a rationale for a Christian rite of passage to adulthood. The first chapter seeks to explain the dynamics of the passage as a time of human growth; it also introduces the rites that function in assisting persons through their passage. The second chapter focuses more narrowly on initiation rites as they have been developed in many cultures to help bridge the gap and activate the transformation from childhood to adulthood. The third chapter cites several models of initiation found in the scriptures. The fourth chapter focuses more specifically on Christian initiation, describing some options now being followed by many churches and sketching the story of Christian initiation from the first century to the twentieth.

Part Two of the book is a report of our experience in creating a contemporary rite of passage to Christian adulthood. The fifth chapter describes the confused world of adolescence, a veritable wilderness without reliable landmarks to assure the travelers toward adulthood that they are on the right track. The sixth chapter introduces the reader to the congregation that entered that wilderness to prepare a more secure way to reach adulthood. The final chapter of the book is the account of our rite of initiation; step by step we move from the moment of separation from childhood to the powerful rite of incorporation.

The Initiation to Adulthood at First Church is still evolving—always changing to fit the distinctive characteristics of each Initiation Group and its individual initiates. The program reported here is a compilation of four separate experiences that I have shared with four separate groups. It includes just a bit of that ideal experience which has been and is being created in my mind and heart and soul, which someday will be enfleshed.

I give only what has been given me. I give with the hope that young people in our culture may be given back a lost rite, the Initiation to Adulthood.

Part One

CHAPTER ONE

Passages and Their Rites

More than twenty-five centuries ago, the prophet Hosea spoke words of warning and wisdom to the people of Israel. In the midst of his passionate pleading with them to forsake their sinful ways and return to their loving God, Hosea proclaimed a view of creation that applies to all God's creatures.

> Come, let us return to the Lord;
> for he has torn, that he may heal us;
> he has stricken, and he will bind us up.
> After two days he will revive us;
> on the third day he will raise us up,
> that we may live before him.
>
> —Hosea 6:1-2

Anyone who has lived deliberately enough to be conscious of life's changing rhythms knows the truth of which Hosea spoke. We are being torn apart constantly, only to be made whole again. We are smitten with devastating force, only to be bound together in a creative process that we only partially comprehend. Sometimes these moments of break-down and break-through occur because we invite them. At other times they occur because of external events over which we have no control. But usually they happen because something within us and without tells us that the time is coming when the old realities and structures will be inadequate. They must be broken so that the new life may come forth.

There are a multitude of examples and illustrations for this growth process. One of the most helpful is that of the lobster, which cannot grow without shedding its shell. In the early years of development, a lobster sheds its shell several times a year. When the lobster reaches maturity, the process continues, though less often. If the process ever stops, the lobster not only ceases to grow, it ceases to live.

Anyone who has chosen that delicious crustacean for dinner knows that the lobster's identity is expressed through that hard exterior shell. To live without that shell involves a period of incalculable risks. But to avoid the risk would mean to cease to live, for the shell is not the lobster. The lobster is the pliable, more vulnerable organism that resides within. And so the abandoned shell is left on the ocean floor as the lobster continues to live out its life with all of its risks.

The process of molting, which is the biologist's term for "shell shedding," has been studied, so its frequency and duration are known. Mature male lobsters molt once a year in the summer or fall. Mature female lobsters molt every other year. It takes twenty minutes to shed a shell. It takes from six to eight weeks of perilous wandering for the new shell to form. The new shell will be a bigger and better variation of the abandoned one.

Human personality develops in stages somewhat like the lobster, but with several significant differences. The frequency and duration of change are not as predictable. We do not know whether an impending transformation will occur suddenly or gradually. We do not know if it can be planned and ordered, or if it will come upon us unexpectedly. We do not know if the new self waiting to be born on the other side of the transition will be a bigger and better variation of the present self. We do not know if we are scheduled for a minor adjustment in life style or a major shift in our being.

But like our crustacean friends, we are involved in a life

process that includes a continuous process of shedding the past and waiting for the future. We continually build structures that give us security and identity. As we grow, however, we realize that those structures are inadequate. And so we abandon them—along with all the comfort and self understanding they offered—and venture out into the unknown.

The Nature of Life's Passages

We begin a journey, a passage. We cross a threshold, enter a state of liminality. (The word "liminality" is derived from the Latin word *limen,* which means threshold.) Once in this liminal state, we can no longer be identified in terms of our past involvements and projects; we have passed out of the familiar, with its known points of reference and safety. We are at sea with ourselves and our world.

This is a time of crisis. The etymology of the word takes us back to the Greek word *krises,* which means decision. The dictionary definition tells us that crisis "is a stage in a sequence of events at which the trend of all future events, especially for better or worse, is determined." The Chinese word for crisis combines two symbols. If taken alone, the one symbol means opportunity; the other, danger.

Life's passages are times of decisive change, with possibilities for better and for worse. They are times of great opportunity—and of great danger.

Opportunities that Accompany Passages

The opportunities are so many that it is impossible to list them all, but it is necessary to mention the most important.

Passages are a time of growing physically and personally. When the restrictive shell is abandoned, the pliable self can move more quickly, can stretch and feel the freedom of being unencumbered by the weight of all that self-protection. Furthermore, there is a new receptivity within the self that allows for and even invites new infusions of energy. And this contributes to growth, for the human being is an energy system in continual creation, caught up in an eternal rhythm of self-destruction and self-construction.

Paradoxically, during these times of passage, the self can grow by opening up to new possibilities and by limiting itself to those most promising. Both directions must be honored, for both bring with them the fullness of life. Either one without the other will cripple the self and disturb the circles in which that person lives.

When one passes over the threshold into the unknown, there is often a flooding of new possibilities. The repertoire of self-perceptions expands, the mindscape seems boundless, and a multitude of never-envisioned or previously-discarded realities present themselves and invite participation. The barriers that separated one from the other are broken down, and with the breakdown comes a breakthrough to a "new heaven and a new earth."

We need to see that new heaven and that new earth from time to time, for without a vision, life on this earth becomes mundane and parochial. We need those perspectives with all of their symbolic variety in order to break out of the drab, one-dimensional self-limitations that we construct for ourselves. Several students of liminality have pointed out that one of the primary characteristics of this state is the capacity to see the self in new and broader and more appropriate perspectives.

> Major liminal situations are occasions on which . . . a society takes cognizance of itself, or rather, where, in an interval between their incumbrancy of specific fixed positions, members of the society may obtain an approximation, however limited, to a global view of [our] place in the cosmos and [our] relations with other classes of visible entities.[1]

In these periods of passage, one can look back at the land that has been left and see its flaws. With that vision one can develop the critical capacities that any person and society

20

require in order to apply the necessary correctives to stay on the right course.

And so, liminality is a time of opening up that allows for growth. It is also a time of limiting, also necessary to growth. The human psyche cannot sustain all the possibilities that the human mind can envision. In order to live with any effectiveness, therefore, we must make decisions. Often the most important decisions are made in times of passage.

To decide means to determine what you will *not* do. We know this by looking at our own lives and the lives of others who share their decision making with us. We also know this by looking at the root of the word "decision." The word is an offspring of the Latin word *decidere,* and the French word *decider.* It means both "to cut off" and "to fall off." A related word is "deciduous," describing those trees which continue to grow only if they drop their leaves to allow for new growth.

When we humans decide, we are like the deciduous tree. We let fall some of the possibilities for our lives and bring all the energy, which was previously dissipated in many areas, to bear on the new growth that we sense within ourselves. Only by making many and often difficult decisions can we focus our energy and our attention, thus giving our commitments strength and significance.

Making decisions is always difficult. It is natural to mourn "the road not taken." But making decisions during times of passage is particularly difficult. The signs, the landmarks, the reference points, the structures that we had before embarking on our passage, have been discarded, and we have to rely on inner resources to take the place of those external verifications. This is frightening. But it also presents a rare opportunity to be exposed to the depths of the soul and to develop religious sensitivities.

Arguments now rage about whether we humans have evolved beyond the stage of hearing inner voices and having original experiences. The arguments can best be used, not to answer the question, but to guide those courageous souls who

21

are willing to enter the unknown around and within them to discover the answer for themselves.

To do this we must become defenseless, vulnerable, weak, willingly stripped of whatever status and authority we have acquired over the years. Then, in the weakened condition, we wait until strength is renewed so we can fly like eagles, if we want, or walk like humans, if that is the way we wish to manifest our new power.

All this may sound somewhat mysterious, which is precisely the way it should sound, for liminality *is* mysterious. It is a time when religiously sensitive persons from the beginning of time have been exposed to the luminous and given deep knowledge. And cultures, also from the beginning of time, have benefited from the courage of those who dare the perilous journey.

This last point is important. It is no secret that most cultures are hostile to those who dare the passages. These people no longer fit into the molds that society has prepared for them; the "powers and principalities" have great difficulty knowing how to relate to liminal persons who are betwixt and between. In addition to that basic hostility, all societies—even the most conformist and repressive—have a deep awareness that contributions are made to them by those *en passage*.

As mentioned above, societies rely upon recurring experiences of liminality to nurture religious and aesthetic sensitivities. The poet, the artist, the religious genius all develop their special gifts by departing from the norms that prove restrictive and by entering the wasteland to recover the symbols that all societies need in order to flourish. If and when they return, these aesthetes are more likely to be rejected than accepted, but somehow the culture will take the gift of their labors.

One sees examples of this everywhere. We may scoff at the work of artists, poets, playwrights, or choreographers who have wandered into new and unfamiliar territory. But they

22

are not rejected completely. Here and there, those closest to them in style sense the substance of their discoveries and present their own offerings, deriving their fundamental insights from the rejected ones. Only after the original genius has died is he or she honored for bravery. We needed the rejuvenation of our symbols. We needed the corrective that came from their perspective. We needed their example to provide us with the knowledge that, perhaps, we, too, could risk the journey. We benefited, both directly and vicariously.

There is a story told about a microcosmic society that had developed in a prison in South America. In that community there were a handful of devout Christians sprinkled among the hardened criminals. In one way or another, all were there because they did not fit into the restrictive behavior patterns that were established by the ruling military junta. Most of the time the criminals scoffed at the Christians, mocking them for their nonviolent attitudes. But as Easter approached, one of the imprisoned leaders came to a priest and told him that his companions wanted mass to be said on Easter at sunrise. The priest was delighted and immediately invited the prisoner to join him at the service. The prisoner laughed, "You damn fool Father. I'm not going to be at your silly mass. I just want to make sure *you* do it. I'll stage a riot at the gates while you worship your God in the cells."

The story reveals much. The dominant society in that prison—like the dominant society most places—depends on those who carry the symbols of eternal truths to do their work, which so often means, simply but profoundly, to have faith. If the symbol bearers do not do their work, the society at large suffers from "symbolic deficiency," to use C. G. Jung's term. It dries up.

There is another reason why society needs people to make the passages appropriate to their lives. Society has authority and responsibility, which must be passed from generation to generation. A person can best accept this authority and responsibility after going through periods of testing and growth. It would be folly to give a young child the authority to drive a car. It would be unwise to give teenagers the responsibility of raising children. It would be foolish to decide to marry after one date. It would be absurd to make a recent college graduate the president of a major corporation. In each case the person needs to mature before he or she is sufficiently competent to manage the responsibility that must be passed on. The way we humans mature is by breaking out of one mode of existence, entering a period of vulnerability, "getting our feet wet," "getting in over our heads," and then struggling until "we get our feet on the ground" and feel the strength and security fit for our new estate. Then, after the passage has been negotiated, society can pass rights and responsibilities.

Dangers that Accompany Passages

Sometimes, we don't make it through our passages. Sometimes the dangers are so great that we become overwhelmed. We let too much of the chaotic element into us or up from within us, and we do not have enough sense of ourselves to handle it all. We come out of the experience either destroyed, or badly scarred, or burdened with a set of unwise decisions made during the time when we were out of control of our lives. Or, we retreat from the experience without ever having lived it through, and return to the securities of our previous existence.

What has happened, very simply but tragically, is that the crisis has presented itself with its full complement of opportunity and danger, but the dangers seemed so great that the opportunities were not pursued.

The Rites of Passage

Primitive cultures—in fact all cultures—have developed rituals to help in times of passage. These rites of passage provide some protection against the dangers. They give some form and structure, some community and sense of historical continuity, some guidance and counsel, which better enable

24

us to cope with the chaos and to derive fullest benefit from the opportunities that accompany the dangers. Furthermore, these rites of passage give some information which we can use to form and reform ourselves for the next stage of our existence; they teach the techniques and mysteries needed to move effectively into the next stage of our existence.

Rites of passage are as numerous as the cultures that have existed upon this globe, but anthropologists and historians of religion find certain similarities among the rites, discernable patterns and recurring rhythms.

Arnold van Gennep, a French anthropologist, has had the greatest influence in the understanding of these rituals with the publication of his 1905 classic, *Les Rites de Passage.* He identified three major stages in these ceremonies: separation (in French, *separation*), transition (*marge*) and incorporation (*agregation*).[2] He associated these rites with liminality, labeling the rites of separation *preliminal* rites, those executed during the transitional stage *liminal (or threshold)* rites, and the ceremonies of incorporation to the new world *post liminal* rites.[3] The complete experience he called the *schema de rites de passage.* His term *schema* usually has been translated as "pattern," although "the flavor of his usage inclines one toward 'dynamics' if such a term might be construed to include 'process' and 'structure.'"[4]

Van Gennep's masterpiece described rites of passage so accurately that his threefold framework is accepted as the most fundamental understanding of what happens in a rite of passage.

The idea of death and rebirth is a second paradigm often used to explain rites of passage. Mircea Eliade, the noted historian of religion, presents this as the central image in his study of initiation rites, entitled *Rites and Symbols of Initiation: The Mysteries of Birth and Rebirth.*

> The majority of initiatory ordeals more or less clearly imply a ritual death followed by Resurrection or a new birth. The central moment of every initiation is represented by the

ceremony symbolizing the death of the novice and his return to the fellowship of the living. But he returns to life a new man, assuming another mode of being.[5]

This movement through death and rebirth can be seen in all the classic moments of passage. At birth the fetus is expelled from the life support system of the mother's womb, passes through the birth canal, and is born as an individual person. At marriage the singularity of the person is destroyed so that "the two become one," a new being; the engagement period is often a time of dramatic self-expansion *and* self-destruction when a new image of oneself as a spouse is developed. At death the person dies and is buried, usually with the assurance that he or she will be born again into a new and fuller life, often after a period of transition.

The mystery of rebirth is found everywhere: in the rhythm of the year, in the wonders of nature, in the miraculous stories of human regeneration, in the development of language. In some cultures the word for womb and tomb is the same. In those cultures the sacred place set aside for the rituals that assist the times of passage is called the womb-tomb.

There is no place where this paradigm is expressed more cogently than in the scriptures.

> What you sow does not come to life unless it dies. And what you sow is not the body which is to be, but a bare kernel, perhaps of wheat or of some other grain. But God gives it a body as [God] has chosen, and to each kind of seed its own body. . . . So it is with the resurrection from the dead. What is sown is perishable, what is raised is imperishable. It is sown in dishonor, it is raised in glory. It is sown in weakness, it is raised in power. It is sown a physical body, it is raised a spiritual body. (1 Corinthians 15:36–38, 42–44)

In speaking of a transformation from a physical body to a spiritual body, or from a thing born of the flesh to a thing born of the spirit, Paul is employing a third traditional way of viewing rites of passage. We move from a lower to a higher nature, from a state of existence that is controlled by impulse and primal drives to a state of existence that is ordered by covenants and social norms. Very often this progression is seen as movement away from the mother, the maternal, and the material, toward the father, the rational, and the spiritual, though such a characterization is flawed by sexist stereotyping.

At birth we leave the mother's womb to begin our increasingly independent life in the world of other humans, in which we must learn compromise and covenanting. At marriage we consciously decide to limit our natural instincts and by means of a carefully considered covenant, we commit ourselves "before God and these witnesses" to love and cherish a selected person. At death we are parted from a material body and take on our spiritual nature, very often with the expectation that soon we shall "dwell in our Father's house."

A final conceptualization of rites of passage involves a dismembering-remembering pattern. At the beginning of the passage, the body is broken and the blood is poured. Then, after a time of testing, the persons are reunited to themselves and to their community as new and more complete beings. They are mysteriously reconstituted. The members of the body are reincorporated. They are re-membered, and are now capable of remembering for they have broken out of the present and traveled deep into the past to the *illo tempore,* the original time, the time of creation, the birth of the universe, and have received their members in "the real way." They have broken out of the mundane and the rational, passed into the other world replete with powerful symbolism, and returned, ready to assume their new and renewed roles in society.

All these different patterns—separation-transition-return, death and rebirth, movement from animal nature to spiritual nature, movement from the instinctual and natural to the rational and cultural, dismembering and re-membering—all

27

are used to explain the passages through which we humans go as we mature. They help to form the rites that are created to facilitate the passages.

We must recognize, however, that periods of passage are highly individualized and complex. They can be periods of major transformation when one's ontological status in life is changed. Sometimes these passages stretch out over several years. Most often they are complex processes. Rarely are they single events.

Inevitably, when rituals are designed to assist persons and societies through these times of passage, there is a tendency to oversimplify them, to reduce the wide variety of human experiences to those common denominators found in the majority, and to repeat them so often that they lose their authenticity and potency. When this happens, someone needs to renew the rites by giving new meaning and vigor to the symbols and by recapturing the essence of mythological material, which mediates the messages of the archaic past. If the rite is left unattended, it will atrophy and die.

This process is clearly visible in our society. Of the classic moments of passage—birth, puberty, marriage, initiation to a spiritual society, death—four still have rites which are constantly being used and reused, criticized and reformed. Baptism, weddings, ordinations and funerals continue to be celebrated, and thoughtful scholars and practitioners continue to raise the most basic questions about their place and purpose in our lives. As those questions are raised and given validity, so new forms are developed to express truths that would have become hidden by unanalyzed usage.

Only the puberty rite has been lost. Over the years it has been so misused and so misunderstood that today we have no valid rite of passage to help children make the treacherous transition into adulthood.

This is a shame. In most societies the initiation rite, as the rite of passage from childhood to adulthood is generally called, was not merely *a* rite of passage, it was *the* rite of passage. It was the cultural keystone of the society, giving strength and form to all other rites. It was the means by which one generation gave to another the basic information of the tribe, the techniques and mysteries of adulthood, the deep truths about birth, sex, marriage, death, the great stories about the gods and supernatural events.

Christian missionaries serving in societies that still have initiation rites realize the effectiveness of those rites. They warn against any attempt to remove them, or—heaven forbid—to replace them with any of the undeveloped rites of present church usage.

> When a church eliminates the initiation rites and fails to provide a substitute for the enculturation mechanism, . . . many of the psychological uncertainties and dark mystery of the West have appeared. Nowadays when the influence of the film industry is being felt in the far corners of the earth, sexy films soon discover the void, and we get another form of delayed reaction. The house swept clean and left empty is now visited by seven spirits.[6]

The missionary in such a society is handicapped, because those to whom he ministers have a working solution to what are unsolved problems in the West.

> These people can say, at least, that young people know their role in life, their sex, their adulthood, their legal status, and their relationship to the spirit world.[7]

The psychological problems of mystery and uncertainty, so common in our society, do not impinge upon them. Any Western advocate of the gospel is therefore at a disadvantage.

The Western young person, who must approach adulthood without such a support system, is at a greater disadvantage than the missionary. Almost all descriptions of life from thirteen to twenty point to the crisis nature of these years. It is a time of great danger. It is also a time of great opportunity.

CHAPTER TWO

Initiation Rites

To those who know about the process of initiation, life is like a mountain with several distinct plateaus connected by labyrinthian trails.

Life's Plateaus

At birth, the newborn are raised up from the earth and allowed to play upon its surface. Then, as they mature, they begin to raise their sights and aspire to higher levels. At a certain moment, they are taken to the place from which the first ascent begins. There they are separated from the children, and shown the path that leads them up to the first plateau, that of adulthood. As they climb the path, they can look back and see where they have been with greater perspective; they can also anticipate where they are going, for they are given the necessary minimal knowledge and taught the necessary minimal skills to enable them to live on the adult plateau. When they arrive at this higher level they will be expected to further their knowledge and refine their skills by living out life as responsible adults.

Some who demonstrate particular knowledge and skillfulness will be selected to go to an even higher plane of existence. They will undergo a journey that bears a marked similarity to the one they have already accomplished. Once again they will be brought to a place where the path leads upward. They will be separated from the other adults and commissioned to climb to new heights, where the elders sit together and deliberate the affairs of state. As they climb, they will be given a body of knowledge and a set of skills necessary for admission into this elite society. When they arrive, they will be expected to expand their knowledge and sharpen their skills by interacting with their new peer group.

If they demonstrate exceptional genius, they may be chosen for one final journey, which will take the climbers to the mountain peak where live the gods and those few mortals who dare to enter into dialogue with them. The ascent to these heights is always the most lonely and perilous. The knowledge and skills for living at these rarified heights must be found within the reservoir of personal resources, which has been filled by the cumulative life experience at each of the lower levels, stretching all the way back to childhood. As they climb to the mountain top, they also wander down through their own depths. As they see new vistas opening up, they also encounter symbolic demons rising up from within. As they feel the exhilaration of victory and new physical conquests passing from one crest onto the next, they also know the prospect of failure and of the psychological destruction that threatens from within.

Many a shaman, modern or primitive, has known the experience of being terrorized by forces raging out of control. Many have dreamed of standing before a dark cave and hearing a summons to enter as they shudder at the thought that they might never come back. Some have not come back; they have gone over the edge of psychosis and have been lost. Those who do make it back will inevitably be scarred, or lamed, or maimed in some way. Yet they bring their broken but victorious selves back to their people. They offer their services to the society. "They fight the demons so that others can hunt the prey and, in general, fight reality."[1]

Part of their service to society is to assume responsibility for initiation to each of the plateaus to which they now return. They are the guides, the gurus, the novice masters, the initiators. They bring children up to adulthood. They take selected adults into the secret society of the elders. They choose some to risk the journey to the summit.

Characteristics of Initiation Rites

Each level demands a special initiation, but all passages have certain similar characteristics. They all involve a series of events: some expand horizons, while others deepen sensitivities; some are very demanding and dangerous, while others are consoling and comforting. These various events remind us that a passage does not occur in an instant. It occurs over an extended period and involves a complex process of maturation and transformation. The specific steps of the initiation help to punctuate and to potentiate the transformation.

Furthermore, each initiation will teach the minimal knowledge and skills, mysteries, and techniques needed to enter the next stage of life. But notice that there is no assumption that *all* mysteries and techniques will be taught. That would be asking too much of the initiation process. The initiates merely need enough to reach the next plateau. Once on it, they will develop further through intentional living.

Each initiation will educate and initiate. The two words reflect two different aspects of the learning process. To educate means literally "to lead out of"; education is derived from the Latin *educare*, to rear or bring up. *Educare* is formed from two Latin words, *ex* (out of) and *ducere* (to lead). To initiate means literally "to go into"; initiation is likewise derived from two Latin words, *In* (in) and *ire* (to go). Education implies a journey outward to new frontiers, an expansion of the self, a broadening of the horizons. Initiation implies a journey inward to the depths of the soul, the innermost secret parts of the heart; it calls for a consolidation of the self, a deepening of the sensitivities.[2] The two modes of knowing may seem contradictory. In fact they are complementary.

All initiation rites, to whatever plateau, follow the same rhythm. They begin with a moment of separation. They end with a moment of re-incorporation. In between is perilous passage.

Initiation to Adulthood

Our concern is for the puberty rite, which takes children to adulthood, and is known universally as *the* rite of Initiation.

The Rite of Separation

One of the most striking features of the puberty rite is the act of separation. Frequently it is physically brutal. Always it is psychologically traumatic. A prototypical separation rite begins when the boys are led blindfolded to a dark hut in the deepest part of the forest. Their parents follow, the mothers mournfully waiting the pending death of their sons as they walk along the sacred path. Then, suddenly the boys are snatched away and taken into the hut. A dull chopping sound is heard from within. Then fearful cries . . . and silence. Solemnly a sword or spear, dripping with blood, is delivered to the mother with some hairs from the boy's head, which allegedly was carried off by the devils. The mothers weep and wail through the night, crying that the devil has murdered their children.[3]

In many cultures the separation involves considerable pain. A tooth, almost always an incisor, is knocked out, or an incision is made into the skin, to create a permanent mark of identity and to give a quantity of blood to be used in creating the new society among the initiates, often known as blood brothers.

These rites of separation teach a number of powerful lessons to all participants—to children, to parents, to the initiates, to those who stand and watch. They teach that the

33

child is dead—that a decisive time in life has come that will involve pain and self-destruction in order to allow growth and self-development. Furthermore, the rites teach that the old ties—the natural ties between mother and child with all that they connote—are now broken. Blood, which accompanied the passage from the mother's womb, will now be drawn from the initiate to demonstrate self-sufficiency and to give the means by which to seal the covenant that will bind the initiates into a community, the new society.

The creation of this new society is a fundamental part of the separation rite. The initiates are to be bound together for life, not merely for the duration of their initiation. Strong emotional ties are supposed to develop among age-mates, who will be newly created together during their initiation ordeals. Those emotional ties can be established only if the ties to the parents are broken.

The Journey into Understanding

Once the rite of separation is concluded and the new society of initiates is created, the second part of the drama begins: the transition from the old to the new. This usually involves a period of testing. The duration of this period varies greatly. Sometimes it is as short as a few days—three being the classic number. Often it is a matter of weeks or months. Sometimes it consumes several years. Almost always there is some flexibility to allow the novice masters to adjust the experience to the personalities of the initiates and to the corporate personality of the initiation group.

During this period, the initiates are expected to get minimal skills and knowledge about four broad subjects: society, sexuality, spirituality, and the self. These four areas include, in one way or another, most of the wisdom that has been gathered in the history of the human race. The initiation is not expected to teach everything—only those minimal techniques and mysteries necessary to enter the next phase of life. The initiates could not possibly learn everything at once.

34

They do not yet have enough life experience to know how to ask the questions. They certainly could not hope to comprehend the answers.

In addition to imparting knowledge, the initiation is expected to effect change—both by symbolically expressing the changes that inevitably occur as the body grows and the person matures, and by mysteriously empowering the transformation. Elaborate sacramental theologies are written to explain this mystery, but inevitably it remains beyond our human understanding. We cannot explain what happens, but we know that it does. When we participate in a marriage, we can feel that strange transformation occurring on many levels. On a superficial level, the ceremony signals to the couple and to the community that the persons who used to be two are now bound together as one; at a deeper level the spirit of the ceremony inexplicably affects the bonding.

The ways by which an initiation rite can empower the transformation from childhood to adulthood are as numerous as the societies with initiation rites, but some common themes emerge. After the ritual of separation, which marks the death of the child in the initiate, the group is taken back to the beginning of time. Each member regresses to the moment of creation—there to witness the cosmogony and to relive the creation of the spirits, the tribe, the family, and, finally the self. They enter into the chaos that precedes form. They see the demons that give the world dynamism but that also threaten to turn into devils capable of breaking everything in two. (The word "diabolical" literally means "to break in two, to destroy.") They begin to appreciate the need for structure through which the dynamics of the past can flow, and they participate in the discovery of the symbols that will hold things together. (The word "symbolical" is the opposite of diabolical; it means "to throw or hold together.")

In this return to the beginning of time, the initiates usually are confronted with a reality that is more than they can handle; for a critical period of time, there is a serious threat to

35

their stability—and perhaps even to their existence. In this period, the adult guides seek to steady them with their presence and with the knowledge of the *communion sanctorum,* the community of saints, which includes all those in the history of the tribe—all those who have been to this frightful place and in this awesome time and have survived it. At this time, also, the guides can begin the instruction in decision-making and assist the initiates to make some of the most fundamental decisions of their lives. As has been mentioned, to make a decision means to determine what *not* to do. When one is overwhelmed by life's possibilities, one must decide which of the many possibilities will be ignored and which will be pursued. Only if this is done can the potential inherent in the self be realized.

This paradigm for learning—opening one's self to many possibilities and then limiting one's self to that which seems most characteristic of the self—will be followed for all four areas in which learning must occur: society, sexuality, self, and spirituality. Let us look at each of those four areas, one at a time.

Society The classic manner of teaching about society is to travel through darkness back to the time when fierce and threatening giants walked freely upon the earth. Very often, as the tales of these fiends are being told, they will suddenly appear in the form of masked intruders and terrorize the initiates into full appreciation of their presence, both then and now. Once the reality of these monsters is fully impressed upon the imagination of the initiates, there is a decisive change in the drama. The Original Ancestors enter the scene armed with power and cunning—frequently assisted by one or two benevolent gods. The ancestors cut into the chaos and create a new culture out of it, usually circumscribing the community with a covenant that separates this tribe from all others.

Once the initiates have regressed to the beginning of time

and witnessed the creation of the culture, they can travel through history, channeled in such a way that they pass through the pools of energy that have invigorated their people since the beginning. They are told the stories of the heroes. Then they relive the heroic deeds that have made their people unique. In so doing, they appropriate to themselves the heroic characteristics honored by their people.

Sexuality To foster their development the initiates are led to experience the fullness of themselves as bisexual beings. The belief is that

> the novice has a better chance of attaining to a particular mode of being—for example, becoming a man or a woman—if [one] first symbolically becomes a totality. For mythical thought, a particular mode of being is necessarily preceded by a *total* mode of being. The androgyne is considered superior to the two sexes just because it incorporates totality and hence perfection.[4]

In one way or another, therefore, initiates are allowed and encouraged to live out both sides of their sexuality. They wear the other's clothes or hair style. They are given—symbolically, of course—the other's genitalia with the accompanying social prerogatives. In experiencing that which is alien, the initiate gets a taste of what it would be like to live life subject to a different set of cultural norms. Additionally, the novice often gets in touch with the deep-seated ambivalence toward the other sex, both the hostility and fear of that which one is not and the attraction and envy of that which one does not have.

It is well known that the ritual of circumcision is a common component of initiation rites. What is not well known is that many initiations include a ritual of subincision, involving a cut immediately below the male genitals. It is widely argued that the act of subincision provides a way for males to experience the birthrights of females: the vagina with its mysterious and enticing yet menacing caves; the capacity to create life; the phenomenon of menstruation, which provides a clear marker point to sexual maturation not offered by the male anatomy.

Once the initiates have experienced their full bisexuality, they are brought to the point of decision. They cut off that part of their life which is unbecoming to their natural sexual state and they become fully male or fully female. It is at this point, that the act of circumcision generally occurs.

In a similar manner, the neophytes are taught the appropriate sexual ethic for their people, which is most often that of monogamy. First there is a period of free exploration; initiation rites are frequently marked by considerable sexual license. Then follows a period of total abstinence, which is seen as a way of preparing the initiates to limit their erotic activity to one spouse. In many societies, marriage immediately follows initiation.

Self This model can also be used for developing an appropriate sense of the self. During the initiation the emerging adults are exposed, either actually or ritualistically, to a wide variety of experiences. They are encouraged to entertain as many possibilities for themselves as they can. It is hoped that they will expand this self concept or, expressed differently, enlarge "their repertoire of self perceptions."

Then, at a critical point, they must choose from among the many possibilities the one that seems most compatible with themselves. Sometimes this is done by the initiates, sometimes by the initiators. Always it is done after the gods have been invoked and with the confidence that divine forces are participating in the decision, which is seen as a vocation, a calling, a destiny.

This process of arriving at an acceptable self-definition is often accomplished with the aid of masks. The mask is the persona, the public representation of a personality. There are a finite number of personalities that have been created in the beginning of time by the heroic lives of the ancestors. The number is determined by the number of lives lived heroically and by the number of roles needed to keep society functioning. The roles of the heroes can never be abandoned. They must be passed, therefore, from one generation to another, as the life force of the older manifestation moves to the point of ineffectiveness.

At the time of decision, initiates are allowed to see the several masks presently available. They try them on to know how they feel. Then they select or have selected for them the mask that best fits their personality. Once the mask has been assigned, the wearer of the mask experiences both grief and exhilaration—grief caused by the knowledge of all those options not chosen and exhilaration as the person begins to explore the ramifications and nuances of that unique personality, which now can be fully developed.

A variation of this same theme is the selection of a totem. After reviewing all the known possibilities for life, the initiates select or are assigned a personal totemic spirit, who will guide their existence by giving energy and a self-centering principle.

Note that these masks and totems are not rigid or inflexible. They are elastic, allowing the initiates to develop the subtleties of their individual nature. In some societies, after the initiates have been *assigned* a totem, *they decide* which part of the totem is most precious to them. In this way they retain a considerable control over their destiny.

The selection process differs from culture to culture. The adult leaders play a key role, occasionally by picking autocratically that personality type which fits best into the larger scheme of things—what the tribe needs now. Any decision would eventually prove counter-productive, however, if the adults were insensitive to the uniqueness of the initiate. The selection process works best when the adults set up the realistic options and the initiates make the selection . . . with the assistance of the gods.

The presence of the gods in this all-important act is

manifest in a number of different ways. Spiritual disciplines are taught to the novices, who pass through periods of fasting, prayer, solitary meditation, and sleep deprivation. All these disciplines demonstrate and develop the capacity of the initiate to transcend the natural, to conquer the appetites of childhood, and to exist on a higher level where will power and spiritual fortitude are required.

The fasting, prayer, solitude, and sleep deprivation also tend to alter normal states of consciousness just enough for the initiates to get a sense of the movement of the unconscious—out of which come the visions and voices that lead to self-awareness and self-definition. The lonely puberty watch is the central feature of the initiation of many North American Indians. The candidates go off alone, where they fast and stay awake to prove their worthiness. They continue this effort until they dream of a certain plant or animal, which is thereby ordained as their guardian spirit. Then they return to the tribe to receive their new name, taken from the plant or animal that will be a guardian spirit eternally. Now they are fully born as a new being. They are ready to live life as responsible adults.

Persons who have experienced solitude can attest to the wisdom of the ancients.

> For a man to take responsibility in public for his society, he must have the deeper integrity to take responsibility in solitude for his own inner life . . . For it is in solitude that the most fearful encounter of all confrontations must take place: facing the emptiness of the self . . . The truth which comes home in solitude is my poverty of being. But an even deeper truth of solitude, if I can accept and affirm my radical poverty of being, is an opening in silence to the mystery of being itself.[5]

Spirituality The initiates' encounter with spirituality occurs at all levels of the initiation. The rite itself is sacred, transporting the initiates out of the mundane existence—now left behind—to a time and place hallowed by its continual use and universal respect. When the initiates learn the ways of

40

their society, they meet the heroic ancestors who have become demi-gods, and they hear the age-old myths that carry the wisdom and the creative energy of the original time into the present. When the initiates are brought to know their sexuality, they discover that sex is fraught with sacredness; it is a way of participating in the mystery of life itself. When they search for their selfhood, either by self-expansion or self-exploration, they know from the examples of those before them and the expectation held out for them, that they may well enter that state of non-being which is the birthplace of every being—indeed of being itself.

During their initiation, they are taught the cultic forms by which their people have always tried to express the eternal realities that lie behind them, and, conversely, by which the eternal forces have sought to impress their existence on temporal beings. But the cultic forms are seen as just that—cultic forms. They are not to be confused with the forces they represent.

In order to protect against just such a confusion, great secrecy surrounds the initiation rite. Initiates are forbidden, on pain of death, to reveal to the uninitiated what happened. Interestingly, the secrecy is advocated because the events are so great and awesome, and because they are so insignificant and ludicrous. As Margaret Mead points out:

> By the time of Initiation the older boys have gradually learned most of the secrets. They know that the voice of the taberan is made by the big bamboo flutes, and may even have learned to play on them . . . that the cassowary, who has been so mysteriously said to swallow little boys, is merely one of the men of a certain clan, wearing a ferocious pair of cassowary-feather eye-pieces, and having suspended from his neck a shell-covered bag in which are stuck two sharpened cassowary bones. . . . To a boy, growing up means finding out that there is no Santa Claus, having it acknowledged that one is old enough to know that all this fanfare and ruffle of drums is a pantomime, devoutly maintained generation after genera-

tion because its maintenance will help to make boys grow, and so promote the well-being of people.[6]

The truth of the matter is that nothing happens in the initiation rite at the very time that everything of significance is happening. There is nothing new under the sun, yet God is making everything new and thereby authentic. Only those who have passed from the naïveté of childhood to the sad and cynical sophistication of adulthood can comprehend this rather distressing truth. They learn it best by coming to know life's absurdities and possibilities, its limits and freedoms, its agony and ecstasy. They learn it best by experiencing its paradoxes and absolutes, by feasting and fasting, by living on the heights and traveling through the depths, by ascending mountain peaks and descending into dark caves, by suffering sensory deprivation and surviving sensory overload.

The Rite of Incorporation

When they have traversed this confusing terrain successfully—constantly moving back and forth to experience its polarities, constantly opening possibilities for life and then deciding on those which bear most personal promise—the initiates finally arrive at a new plateau and are reincorporated into their society.

In this final ritual the initiates frequently are given new names fitting to their new estate in life. Always they are given new status, that accorded to adults. Their return to the community is greeted with feasting and jubilation. There is an undercurrent of sadness, however, as the celebrants recognize the fundamental fact that the innocent children who were separated out and killed off a short time ago are replaced by new beings, sophisticated adults in possession of the most important secrets—even those which speak of life's folly and Santa Claus' death. It is the mothers who live out their sadness most fully, for, in the ritual of incorporation, they usually are ignored by the young adults, whose birth in the spirit has superseded that birth from their wombs.

Rites of Initiation in the Higher Religions

The rite of initiation to adulthood as described in its most rudimentary form has countless variants. Suffice it to say, as Mircea Eliade has said:

> All pre-modern societies, (that is, those that lasted in Western Europe to the end of the Middle Ages and in the rest of the world to the first World War) accord primary importance to the ideology and techniques of initiation.[7]

Furthermore, most of the so-called higher religions have preserved some aspects of the archaic rites of passage to adulthood.

The Hindu Rite: Upanayana

Most Hindu boys in India of the upper three castes, for example, will go through an initiation rite called the *upanayana,* "the beginning of wisdom." The highest caste, the Brahmins, initiate their boys when they are eight years old. The *kschatriya* (soldiers and rulers) and the *vaisyas* (farmers, shopkeepers and merchants), initiate at eleven or twelve years of age.

The young Brahmin is destined to be *dvi-ja,* "twice born." His second birth is effected by a guru, who functions as both mother and father. After a period of preparation, the auspicious day is set for the ritual of separation, which is preceded by a night of silence and marked by a meal of sweet foods served by the mother. This is the last meal he will eat with his mother. A barber arrives to shave the boy's hair, cut his nails, bathe him, and give him new clothes for his journey.

At this point, the emerging man goes to his guru, who, according to some practices, takes him to his womb (home) for three days, after which he will be born again. The birth process begins when the guru puts his hand on the boy's shoulder. This is the moment of conception. Three days later, having been nourished by the wisdom deep within the guru's being, the boy has matured into manhood (at age 8!) and

43

returns to his home for the ritual of reincorporation, which involves the passage of authority from the guru to the student. First the guru gives to the student a sacred cord, a white cotton thread of three strands, twisted together, the symbol of second birth. He also whispers into the student's right ear the holiest of all verses:

> Let us meditate on the most excellent light of the Creator; may he guide our intellects.

The ritual concludes with a prayer by the young man and a blessing from the old man. Thus a new Brahmin is fully born. On the evening of his second birth, this new being performs the ritual of evening prayer, one of the daily duties of a Brahmin.[8]

The Buddhist Rite: Shinbyu

A Buddhist child in Southeast Asia will experience a similar rite known as the *shinbyu,* through which, at age twelve to fourteen, he relives the renunciation of Buddha. On a certain day he will be clad in the finest silks and fed the most sumptuous foods. After a ride around town on a gleaming white horse, the youngster returns home to find ascetic Buddhist monks waiting for him, clad in their plain yellow robes and distinguished by the shaven heads. They beckon him to come with them to a monastery. The boy removes his bright turban and cloth of silk, allows his hair to be cut and his scalp shaved, and prostrates himself three times before the monks, asking to be permitted to accompany them. The abbot of the monastery gives the novice his own yellow robe, and the monks surround him and take him away.

The next day he returns to his home with other monks. With the beggar's bowl given him at the monastery, he begs food from his own mother, who treats him no longer with maternal concern but with the reverence due a holy man. The novice also has a new name. He has abandoned his family name and is now known as a "son of Buddha" (*sakya-putto*). During his stay in the monastery, the monks will teach him the spiritual disciplines of the way of Buddha, leading to eventual enlightenment. The monks will also teach him to be independent in his thinking and not to accept unquestioningly all that he is told.

The Jewish Rite: Bar Mitzvah and Bath Mitzvah

In Judaism, a boy's childhood ends at age thirteen, when he becomes Bar Mitzvah, a son of the law. Already incorporated into the covenant community by his circumcision, which occurred eight days after his birth, the thirteen-year-old is singled out for an intense period of preparation in which he studies the Hebrew language as a means of learning the ways of his people. On the day designated for his passage to adulthood, he bids goodbye to his mother and is escorted to the altar by several members of the congregation, who read the Torah portion with him. For the first time he wears the *tallit* (prayer shawl) and reads a lengthy section of the Torah and comments upon it. From that point on he is Bar Mitzvah, responsible for his own decisions and expected to interpret for himself the meaning of God's commandments. Soon thereafter he hears his father's tongue-in-cheek blessing appropriate for the occasion:

> Blessed art thou, Lord God, King of the Universe, who now relieves me of care for this child.

Those who become Bar Mitzvah often comment that the experience is arduous; there is a real sense that the boy is on trial. The wisest of rabbis would smile with satisfaction. That's exactly how the experience was envisioned. It is supposed to be arduous. The boy is on trial to demonstrate his skill, ability, and knowledge of the Torah and Judaism itself.

> To the principle, "No taxation without representation," Judaism replies, "No representation without taxation," but the taxation which it envisages is that of the mind and heart. No representation without education.[9]

It is the custom that the Bar Mitzvah will return to the

45

synagogue on the next sabbath to read the prophetic section of the scriptures known as the *haftarah.* This is symbolic of the Bar Mitzvah experience beyond the actual day of the ceremony. The new adult has already demonstrated entry-level knowledge; now he is expected to expand his knowledge and sharpen his skills in his interaction with other adults.

In most of these cultures, only males have a highly developed rite of initiation to adulthood. Occasionally, girls have a rite paralleling that designed for boys, such as the Bath Mitzvah of Judaism, during which a young woman assumes maturity by becoming a daughter of the law.

The Christian Rite: The Lost Rite
Christianity, the tradition from which this author writes, has no single custom of initiation. Rather it has a variety of practices and a rich reservoir of resources and rituals surrounding baptism, confirmation, first communion. It also has a long line of powerful personalities who have undergone initiation, who provide us with models of faithfulness, and models for initiation.

CHAPTER THREE

Scriptural Models of Initiation

It probably comes as no surprise that ideas as archetypal as initiation would be found somewhere in the scriptures. It may be surprising that they are found again and again.

The Initiation of the Patriarchs

Abram/Abraham, Sarai/Sarah

The story of our faith begins with Abraham, who was called to separate himself from all that he had known in Haran and strike out on a journey into the unknown that eventually would bring him to a full and more blessed life.

> Leave your own country, your kinsmen, and your father's house, and go to a country that I will show you . . . I will bless you and make your name so great that it shall be used in blessings (Genesis 12:1–3 NEB).

So Abram went. He took his wife Sarai and began the passage to a new life. As it turned out, the transition was to be a lengthy one. For years he wandered. And as he wandered he surely wondered about his decision to leave the security of his father's home for no children came.

Finally, when Abram was ninety-nine years old, God came to him and said:

> I am God Almighty. Live always in my presence and be perfect, so that I may set my covenant between myself and you and multiply your descendants (Genesis 17:1–24 NEB).

As part of the covenant, God changes the names—the essences—of both Abram and Sarai. He became Abraham—not merely father, but father of a multitude. She became Sarah—a true princess. They had successfully negotiated the passage to a new state of existence. Shortly thereafter, Sarah bore a son, Isaac, the first of a long line of descendants.

But the nature of life is that no one passage is ever sufficient. The shells of security constantly must be broken and discarded to allow the soul to grow. When Abraham was an old man and his son Isaac a boy-man, God resolved to take father and son on another journey to a deeper level of existence.

Isaac

One night, a strange voice from deep within Abraham spoke:

> Take your son, Isaac, your only son, whom you love, and go to the land of Moriah (an unknown place) and offer him as a sacrifice on one of the hills which I will show you (Genesis 22:2 NEB).

Abraham woke from his sleep and did as he was told. He took Isaac, separating him from his mother and his home, and walked for three days. Finally they arrived at the mountain. Father and son went to the top, ostensibly to complete the task begun when the boy was separated from his mother and his home. Abraham built an altar and arranged the wood. He bound his son Isaac and laid him on the altar on top of the wood. Then he stretched out his hand and took the knife to kill his son. Only then, at the last moment, did the voice of

God come again to Abraham, stopping him from filicide, returning the son to the father, and renewing the covenant made many years before.

> This is the word of the Lord: by my own self I swear: inasmuch as you have done this and have not withheld your son, your only son, I will bless you abundantly and greatly multiply your descendants until they are as numerous as the stars in the sky and the grains of sand along the seashore (Genesis 22:16–17 NEB).

The rite of passage over, father and son—now strengthened by their ordeal—returned home to be reincorporated into the normal flow of their lives.

But when they returned home, they were different, stronger, more secure. They had passed through an experience that had brought them to an encounter with death and with God. Now they possessed a deep knowledge and a strange power they didn't have before the ordeal: they had been born again.

Jacob/Israel

We see a similar movement in the life of Isaac's son Jacob, who encountered the terror of life and death when he passed through the water of the river Jabbok. (See Genesis 32:22–32 NEB.)

In order to achieve his maturity, Jacob leaves his family, goes off alone, is immersed in the living waters of the Jabbok, encounters the unknown in the form of a man—or an angel, or devil, or God. (Translations of the Hebrew word differ.) Jacob engages this mysterious being in a life-and-death struggle. By the end of the battle, Jacob has been transformed into a new being. He has been lamed. He has also been renamed. That old, conniving, scheming child named Jacob is dead. Israel now lives. At the moment of his rebirth, Israel looks up and sees his brother Esau coming toward him in order that the family might be reunited.

Joseph

The opportunity-burden of initiation would next fall upon Israel's favorite son Joseph, who, as a young man, was separated from his brothers in an act that was intended to cause his death, but, because of the transforming power of God, brought him to new life in Egypt. Decades later, after experiencing the extremes of plenty and famine, of feasting and fasting, of the depths of the prison and the exalted heights of Pharaoh's court, Joseph was reunited with his family and blessed by his aging father with the full authority of heaven and hell:

> "So may God almighty bless you with the blessings of heaven above, and the depths that lurk below, the blessings of the breast and the womb, and the blessings of your father" (Genesis 49:25 NEB).

The transition is complete. Joseph, who was forced out of the family and thought dead, had survived his ordeal, had returned to the family to receive the blessings and authority from his aging father.

The Initiation of Moses

A similar journey was undertaken by Moses. In the process of maturing, beginning the search for his true identity, experiencing previously unknown surges of power—both physical and political—Moses committed a murderous act and found it necessary to break with the home in which he had been raised. He fled to the wilderness and settled in the land of Midianites—commonly identified as one of the tribes of the Kenites, descendants of the outcast Cain and the blacksmiths of the desert. The Kenites befriended this outcast, providing him a home, a wife, and an introduction to their cultic practices, which most likely included an initiation rite and surely involved a deep respect for the gift of fire, "very probably considered a divine power."[1]

Moses' first meeting with the people of Midian took place at a well where some shepherds attempted to drive off the daughters of Jethro as they sought to water their sheep. But Moses, following a classic initiation practice, "took the girls' part and watered their sheep himself" (Exodus 2:17 NEB), thereby experiencing, at least in part, the social role prescribed for the opposite sex. Because of that auspicious beginning, Moses was invited to take up residence in the home of the priest who soon became his father-in-law.

Under the tutelage of this unique and mysterious figure—called variously Reuel, Jethro, and Hobab—Moses learned the rhythms of nomadic life. As he tended the sheep, he spent many hours in silence and solitude, until he received a vision—fittingly for one trained in the ways of the Kenites—of a burning bush. He heard a voice from the bush identifying itself, not merely as the fire deity worshiped by the Midianites, but as the God of history, who was in the process of creating a new people from the children of Israel.

> I am the God of your forefather, the God of Abraham, the God of Isaac, the God of Jacob. . . . I have indeed seen the misery of my people in Egypt. I have taken heed of their sufferings, and have come down to rescue them from the power of Egypt, and to bring them up out of that country into a fine, broad land. . . . Come now; I will send you to Pharaoh, and you shall bring my people Israel out of Egypt (Exodus 3:6–8, 10 NEB).

The Initiation of the People of Israel

With this grand vocation indelibly imprinted in his mind, Moses returned to the people of Israel as a new being, vested with a spiritual power without equal in his time. Using his own experience among the Midianites, including the rhythms and rituals of an initiation rite, he helped to forge a corporate personality out of the descendants of Jacob, thereby initiating the whole people of Israel into a new way of life.

The first act of the drama was the separation from the land of their birth and the state of slavery to Egyptian masters. In the presence of the avenging angel of death the Israelites began their journey, immersed themselves in water by passing through the miraculously opened Red Sea, thereby experiencing firsthand the nature of the crisis. The water was dangerous, threatening them with death. The water was also promising; it led them to freedom. When the Israelites emerged safe on the other side they followed the pattern of initiates in every culture. With singing and dancing and general rejoicing that the Egyptian "horse and his rider has been thrown into the sea" they formed a new society out of the former slaves.

Throughout their history, the poets and prophets of Israel will remember that miraculous passage. Isaiah includes the remembrance in a prayer of petition.

> Awake, awake, put on your strength,
>   O arm of the Lord,
> Awake as you did long ago, in days gone by.
> Was it not you
>   who dried up the sea, the waters of the
>   great abyss,
> And made the ocean depths a path for the
>   ransomed?
>
> —Isaiah 51:9-10 NEB

Now the first act in the drama had passed. The Israelites had been dramatically separated from their past. They had crossed the threshold and entered the liminality of the desert. But they were nowhere near the promised land. A period of trial and testing began at this point. The children of Israel wandered in the wilderness for forty years, suffering hunger and thirst, giving up hope, losing their sense of direction as well as their sense of themselves. When their spirits reached their nadir and they murmured against Moses and Aaron that they would rather be back at the fleshpots of Egypt, secure in their slavery, Yahweh finally called Moses to the heights of Mt. Sinai and the people vicariously experienced a ritual with many classic initiation motifs.

With the counsel of his mysterious mentor, the priest and father-in-law, Moses circumscribed the sacred mountain, prohibiting anyone to touch it on penalty of death. Then, because of the providential movement of Yahweh, and possibly with the skillful assistance of the ever-helpful Kenites, a great pandemonium broke loose, complete with lightning (the Hebrew word is *lappid,* usually translated "torches") and thunder (the Hebrew word is *quoloth,* usually translated "noises" or "voices"), and trumpets (surely the shofar with its eerie, piercing sound).[2]

Now that the people were appropriately intimidated, they were commanded to observe ceremonies of sanctification involving ritual washing and sexual abstinence. Then Moses passed through the thunder and lightning and smoke and was given the code of laws by which the Israelites were to order their lives. He stayed on the mountain top for three days, after which he returned to the people to tell them of the covenant he had received on the heights, to instruct them in the preparation of burnt offerings and peace offerings, and to take blood from those sacrifices and mark the people with it. "Behold the blood of the covenant which the Lord has made with you" (Exodus 24:8). Moses again returned to the mountain, now for seven days, followed by still a third time, for forty days, during which he neither ate bread nor drank water. When he descended from this final visit to the heights, the skin of his face shone almost like a mask—the mask of God's glory. (See Exodus 34:29–35.) It was then that Moses renewed the covenant for the people, renamed them as God's people, and led them on to the Promised Land.

With the death of Moses and the entry into the promised land, the paradigm was fully established. The people—not as individuals, but as a society—were instructed to relive the Exodus each year, dying to their slavery in Egypt, passing through the water of the Red Sea into the unknown of the Sinai, and recovenanting themselves enroute to the eternal promises. In this history, other leaders—from Joshua to Jonah—would undergo similar transformations. Each male would undergo the ritual of circumcision as a way of tying his individual identity to that of the corporate personality. But the most significant acts of initiation would always be the re-enacting and remembering of the Exodus.

Initiation in the Life of Jesus

For Christians, the most significant acts of initiation emerge not in the Exodus, but in the life of Jesus of Nazareth, whom we believe to be the promised Christ. The stories of his life—from birth through death to resurrection—are filled with initiation motifs.

The Nativity
Jesus' birth was surrounded by a multitude of paradoxes. Elizabeth, an old and barren woman, gave birth to a child. Zechariah was struck dumb in order to be given wisdom. Mary rejoiced that God had pulled the mighty from their thrones and had exalted the lowly, had filled the hungry and sent the rich empty away. (See Luke 1:46–55.) Joseph, engaged to marry Mary, resolved to break the engagement, when he was visited by an angel instructing him to renew the covenant (Matthew 1:19–21). The shepherds were filled with fear before they could have room in their being for the news of great joy (Luke 2:9). The wise men visited the agent of death, King Herod, who unwittingly directed them to the source of light and life (Matthew 2:1–8). In the midst of all this, the Word, who was in the beginning with God and through whom all things were made, became flesh and began to live out an earthly existence (John 1:1–5).

The Visit with the Elders
We know nothing about Jesus' childhood or what would

54

now be called his adolescence, with one interesting exception.

When Jesus was twelve years old, his parents went to Jerusalem, as was the custom, to celebrate the feast of the Passover.

> When the feast was ended, as they were returning, the boy Jesus stayed behind in Jerusalem. His parents did not know it, but supposing him to be in the company they went a day's journey, and they sought him among their kinsfolk and acquaintances; and when they did not find him, they returned to Jerusalem, seeking him. After three days they found him in the temple, sitting among the teachers, listening to them and asking them questions; and all who heard him were amazed at his understanding and his answers. And when they saw him they were astonished; and his mother said to him, "Son, why have you treated us so? Behold, your father and I have been looking for you anxiously." And he said to them, "How is it that you sought me? Did you not know that I must be in my Father's house?" And they did not understand the saying which he spoke to them. And he went down with them and came to Nazareth, and was obedient to them; and his mother kept all these things in her heart.
>
> And Jesus increased in wisdom and in stature, and in favor with God and man (Luke 2:41–52).

The points of contact between this occurrence and classic rites of initiation are too striking to go unnoticed. The setting is the Passover—the annual occasion when the Jews relived their Exodus from Egypt, their corporate initiation rite. The boy's age is twelve, often the age of first initiation. The child is separated from his parents and spends three days in the temple conversing with the elders. When finally discovered and questioned by his mother, he reproves her: "Did you not know that I must be in my Father's house?" (Luke 2:49). She is puzzled by his behavior and seeming rejection. She has no choice but to do as the mothers of initiates in every culture: she "kept all these things in her heart" (Luke 2:51). Mary becomes silent with the foreboding knowledge that her child is being taken from her.

It needs to be mentioned that there is no known evidence of puberty initiation rites having been practiced in Judaism at the time. Circumcision, the rite of entry into the covenant community, had become a custom related to infancy. It was performed traditionally on the eighth day of the child's life as a way of guaranteeing that at no time would the Jewish child be outside the community of the faithful. The Bar Mitzvah was developed in the 14th century.[3] But even though Jesus' experience was no puberty initiation rite, the paradigm is deep within the soul and so behavior appropriate to initiation is manifest.

The Baptism

This same phenomenon is evident in the next recorded event in the life of Jesus of Nazareth: his baptism by John. Two fundamental initiation motifs surface:

● The baptism, a water rite of cleansing and purification, wherein the submersion into the watery chaos is followed by an emergence to new life in the spirit.

● The voice of God, which calls Jesus to his special vocation and gives him his unique self-consciousness.

The Call to Initiation

Throughout his ministry, Jesus continually lives out or speaks about his initiation. He spends forty days and nights in the wilderness, where he fasted and was tempted by the devil, where "he was with the wild beasts, and the angels ministered unto him" (Mark 1:13 NEB). He leaves his family of birth to create a new society of disciples. Once, when his mother and sister came to take him back home, he demonstrates how thoroughly he had broken those ties by exclaiming:

"Who is my mother? Who are my brothers?" and pointing to the disciples, he said, "Here are my mother and my brother. Whoever does the will of the heavenly Father is my brother, my sister, my mother" (Matthew 12:48–30 NEB).

He advised the rich young man to break his ties with home in order to enter the Kingdom of God. He admonished Nicodemus to be born again, to open himself to spiritual birth—different and more complete than birth from the water—if he was to see the Kingdom of God. When the people wanted a sign, Jesus told them the only sign he would give was the sign of Jonah, the prophet who had lived in the belly of a whale for three days before being offered up with new life, one that now was consistent with the vocation that God had established for Jonah. He announced his own passion in terms clearly reminiscent of a passage:

> The Son of Man will be delivered to the chief priests and doctors of the law; they will condemn him to death and hand him over to a foreign power. He will be mocked and spat upon, flogged and killed; and three days afterward he will rise again. . . . [This is] the cup that I will drink . . . the baptism that I am baptized with (Mark 10:33–34, 39 NEB).

In each instance, Jesus was living out the patterns of initiation.

Jesus as Initiator

Jesus also functioned as the initiator, the novice master, the one who has gone to the depths and the heights, received the spiritual wisdom, and then returned to the world to teach what he has learned. He often goes off alone, to be rejuvenated through prayer. He taught through stories and actions, and often asked those who heard him to keep silence. He created a new society among disciples by separating them from their families. Once, he selected three disciples to go with him to the top of a sacred mountain.

> [He] led them up a high mountain apart. And he was transfigured before them, and his face shone like the sun, and his garments became white as light (Matthew 17:1–2).

Moses and Elijah appeared. A bright cloud overshadowed them. And a voice spoke to them. The disciples fell on their faces in awe, and when they looked up, only Jesus remained. As they were coming down the mountain, Jesus gave them the traditional injunction of secrecy: "Tell no one the vision" (Matthew 17:9).

The occasion when Jesus most clearly assumed the functions of the master of the initiation was the Last Supper. The mood of the upper room, the advice of the final discourses, the act of sharing a simple meal by which he could be remembered—all these are strikingly akin to the final meeting of initiation groups since the beginning of time. Soon the master would leave them. Soon they would return to the cruel world. Now they must accomplish the delicate task of passing authority, spiritual authority, from master to disciple. Let us look more closely at this final meeting in the upper room.[4]

After they had broken bread together, Jesus addressed his followers, beginning the termination proceedings. "My little children," he said, "I am to be with you only a little longer. For your future without me, I leave a legacy. First, I am giving you a new commandment: love one another; as I have loved you, so you must love one another. Furthermore, I promise that if you love me and keep my commandments, then at my request the Father will give you another Paraclete to be with you forever. He is the Spirit of Truth whom the world cannot accept since it neither sees nor recognizes him; but you do recognize him since he remains with you and is within you. The Paraclete, the Holy Spirit that the Father will send in my name, will teach you everything and remind you of all that I have taught you myself" (paraphrased excerpts from John 13:33—14:26).

At this point Jesus interrupts his discourse to make sure his words are being heard and understood. He repeats himself step by step. He will not be with them much longer. He gives them the new, all-encompassing commandment to love one another. If they keep his commandments, he will request the Father to send another Paraclete. He might have explained

58

that a paraclete is literally "one who stands at the side," offering counsel and comfort, even offering to be a spokesman.

Jesus had been a paraclete for his disciples during the years of their time together, separated from their families and their jobs. Now Jesus was going away. They would return to the world, a world hostile to him and to them, a world unable to accept this other Paraclete whom it would never see or recognize. But the disciples would know, for this Spirit of Truth would be with them and within them. From now on, because of the gift of this Spirit, the disciples would have authority over their own lives. The Spirit within them would teach them; reminding them of the teaching of Jesus, but leading them to a personal authoritativeness, as yet unknown to them.

Jesus then bids them farewell, explaining that he *must* go in order for the Paraclete to come to them. Otherwise, the disciples would always depend on the wisdom of Jesus, and never take responsibility for their own lives. Jesus knows so much more than they do ("I have much more to tell you, but you cannot hear it now") but they now know enough to begin the next stage of their life, the time without the Master. He tells them to have courage, leaves them with peace, prays for them and then goes away to suffer the baptism with which he must be baptized. In the words of the Apostles' Creed,

> [Jesus] suffered under Pontius Pilate, was crucified, dead, and buried. He descended into hell. On the third day he rose again and sitteth on the right hand of God the Father, from whence he shall come to judge the quick and the dead.

The disciples return to the world, destroyed by the death of their Master and forever scarred by the vision of his suffering, but also empowered with a spiritual dynamism and vested with the authority to go forth and make all nations disciples by baptizing persons everywhere in the name of the Father and of the Son and of the Holy Spirit. Consequently from the

59

earliest days of Christianity the sacrament of baptism became the way by which all persons were initiated into the community of faith. If the contemporary church has any hope of rediscovering or recreating a Christian rite of initiation, it must take stock of where it is and look carefully at where it has been in its understanding and practice of baptism.

CHAPTER FOUR

Initiation in the Christian Tradition

The contemporary Christian church is in a confused state about the appropriate way to initiate its young into adulthood. Out of the confusion come two responses—conversion and confirmation—both of which fault in their understanding of the age. Conversion tends to exploit the turbulent psychosocial dynamics of the teenage years. Confirmation tends to shy away from the turbulence, often offering a rather insipid welcome into a not-so-secret or elite society, the local congregation.

Conversion

Conversion has traditionally been a rite of passage for the more evangelical Christians. A number of factors in universal human development, coupled with a vacuum in the society at large, conspire to make teenagers ripe for Christian conversion:

- There is an inrushing or outpouring of sexual feelings, which can easily be termed as sinful in our society.

- There is also the inevitable role confusion that develops as children search among the options of adulthood for some acceptable personality configuration.

61

- Finally there is the sometimes overwhelming need to be affirmed by adults and accepted into the world of adults.

To respond to these needs, the evangelicals follow a strategy guiding the emerging adult to a moment of decision; they speak directly to the plight of the adolescent in words such as:

- Your sexuality is truly proof of your inherent sinfulness, but you can come out of that state of sin, be washed in the blood of the Lamb and become new in Christ Jesus.

- Your confusion about yourself and your future is proof that you must make decisions; therefore we offer you the once-in-a-lifetime chance to make the choice to end all choices. We invite you to make a decision for Christ.

- And last, but not least, we stand ready to welcome you as fellow travelers along the road that leads to eternal life. As soon as you have made your decision, we invite you to talk with our counselors—all mature in their faith—who will welcome you into your new life.

This characterization of the revival may be a bit simplistic, but the basic thrust is much as described. Using the archetype of the initiation, evangelists direct their appeal to adolescents of every age and invite them into the world of Christian maturity. When the people leave the certainty of their seats and walk the distance to the altar, they are making a passage. When they arrive at the altar, they also arrive at the first stage of adulthood. When they deliver their experiential narrative to the company of believers, they are accepted as adults, perhaps for the first time. Further, conversion often involves a selection of some aspects of one's personality at the expense of others—that is, to be converted means that one has decided to lay aside childhood associations and to embrace the new associations appropriate to adulthood.[1] It is this

62

moment, the decisive moment of life, toward which all Christian nurturing of children is directed, and from which all Christian service as an adult flows.

At one time in our nation's history, the conversion was so important that Sunday School teachers were given systematic instruction in how to prepare a person for this pivotal passage of life. The chart shown on the following pages, developed in 1913 to accompany the *New Convention Normal Manual for Sunday School Workers,* provided a guide to human development leading to and from a "religious crisis" in the intermediate stage, generally thought to come around twelve to fourteen years of age.[2]

This emphasis on juvenile piety in the Sunday Schools contributed to a rising frequency of conversion among young people, but it also contributed to the transient quality of many of these conversions. As social pressures for early conversions increased, many persons found themselves struggling with the memory of a powerful experience that they did not understand and could not correlate with the other realities of their lives. When they were out of the social climate that ripened them for conversion, many persons looked back on their moment of decision and realized it was rather shallow and ineffective, "like a vaccination that did not take." One young adult expressed it in this way:

> As time went on and the enthusiasm began to wane, I was gradually brought to realize that I had undertaken a more difficult task than at first appeared obvious. I had pledged myself to the Christian life without counting the cost. [He puts blame partly on himself and partly on his mentors.] This arose partly from my own ignorance and partly from the extravagant representations of older professors and of my religious teachers generally. The notion that 'experiencing religion' was a miraculously radical change led me, as it has led others, to conclude that if conversion was genuine, the natural propensities and passions would either be eradicated or so neutralized as to be harmless.[3]

PREVIEW OF THE SECOND DIVISION—THE PUPIL

General	The **BEGINNER** is considered as follows:	The **PRIMARY PUPIL** is considered as follows:	The **JUNIOR PUPIL** is considered as follows:
I. PHYSICALLY.			
Energy	1. Restless	1. Active	1. Energetic
Physical Dependence	2. Dependent	2. Less Dependent	2. Growing Independence
II. MENTALLY.			
Attention	1. Attention Brief	1. Attention Growing in Power	1. Voluntary Attention
Curiosity	2. Curiosity	2. Curiosity Strong	2. Inquisitive
Memory	3. Memory but Slightly Developed	3. Memory Rapidly Developing	3. Verbal Memory at Height
Imagination	4. Imagination "Run Riot"	4. Imagination Imitative	4. Imagination Toned Down
III. SOCIALLY.			
Play	1. Plays Alone	1. Plays with Companions	1. Plays with the Gang
Egoism	2. Self Centered	2. Sensitive	2. Social Nature Developing
IV. SPIRITUALLY.			
Religion	1. Impressionable	1. Conversion a Possibility	1. Great Evangelistic opportunity

The **INTERMEDIATE PUPIL** is considered as follows:	The **SENIOR PUPIL** is considered as follows:	The **ADULT PUPIL** is considered as follows:
1. Energy Less	1. Energy Greatly Increased	1. Endurance
2. Self Sufficient	1. Self Reliant	1. Aggressive
1. Voluntary Attention Strengthened	1. Attention to the Point of Application	2. Attention to the Point of Concentration
2. Investigative	2. Independent Thinking	2. Original Research
3. Memory Based on Association of Ideas	3. Logical Memory	3 Philosophical and Practical Memory
4. Imagintive Literature a Delight	4. Imgination Productive of Ideals	4. Imagination Creative
1. Plays with Team	1. Plays as Exhibition Skill and Strength	1. Plays for Recreation
2. Self Conscious	2. Self Sacrificing	2. Service
1. Religious Crisis	1. Choice of Service	1. Life of Service

Confirmation

Many ministers of mainline Protestant churches can look through their own personal histories or those who come to their offices for counsel, and find moments of intense pain and embarrassment suffered because of social pressures for conversion. Consequently they have rejected the merits of the conversion experience and have reacted by offering their young people an opportunity to be confirmed. Unfortunately, most confirmation programs fault as tragically in one direction as conversion "programs" do in the other. Rather than taking seriously the dynamics of adolescence, many confirmation programs disregard them and offer an alternative that is frustrating to the adult leaders and increasingly avoided by those who could be confirmands. As one clergyman put it: "I felt that something special had to be done for thirteen year olds. And I looked to my bag of tricks (the Christian tradition) and all I could find was confirmation."

The word "confirmation" is used to refer to a particular liturgical act, and to a special program of education associated with it. This two-fold reference has existed only since Reformation times. Before then, confirmation denoted only the liturgical act itself.[4] To Roman Catholics and Episcopalians, confirmation is a sacrament. Protestants usually refer to it as an ordinance of the church. The purpose of confirmation is usually stated in some relationship to baptism. It is "the completion of baptism" (Tertullian), or "the renewal of the baptismal vow" (Martin Bucer). Sometimes confirmation is viewed as an induction into military life; Thomas Aquinas called the confirmand a *miles Christi,* a soldier of Christ ready for spiritual combat with evil. Occasionally it is regarded as a kind of graduation ceremony, marking the end of one's Christian instruction, and the reception at the fellowship of the Lord's Supper. In Congregationalism, confirmation derives its meaning in relationship to the act of "owning the covenant."

Owning the covenant was a mark of membership in a particular community. In the course of time three different aspects of covenant were recognized: the covenant of grace, celebrated in infant baptism; the churchly covenant, which admitted a person to the Lord's table and permitted him to vote in the affairs of the church; and the civil covenant, which set the political stance of the community.[5]

In the United Church of Christ, which combines elements of the Reformed, Lutheran, and Congregational traditions, the form of the confirmation program varies greatly

from those who require only one session to those who require more than 100; from those with one student to those with more than fifty; from thirty-minute class sessions to ten-hour sessions; from programs that study the church budget to one that includes a trip to the Holy Land. . . . The 'average' confirmation program is composed of ten thirteen- and fourteen-year-olds and consists of thirty-four class sessions of an hour and twenty minutes in length. . . . In the vast majority of cases, the pastor or assistant plans the confirmation program, and in more than half the programs he or she is solely responsible.[6]

But, in spite of the effort put into confirmation activities, only one out of four ministers is "very satisfied" and most are downright frustrated. Even more distressing is the attitude of adolescents. In an age when teenagers are fascinated by the religions of the East, joining cults, and paying hard-earned money to learn the secrets of transcendental meditation and other spiritual disciplines, there has been a dramatic decline in the number of confirmands. As one Christian educator noted:

Even among those young people who remain related to the church, there are many who admit that confirmation has no lasting significance for them, and some who will denounce the practice as fraudulent.[7]

The Components of Initiation

What has happened? Answers differ, but many seem to point in the same direction. To a great extent we have lost the sense of inter-relatedness of those rites that comprise Christian initiation—baptism, confirmation, first communion. Still more tragic, we are losing the sense that these rites are significantly related to life itself.

Infant baptism is experienced by many as a delightful little ceremony when people get dressed up to smile as a baby cries. It has little to do with crucifixion and resurrection and new life. It has little to do with being torn away from one's natural self with all its selfishness to live a life of service in Christ Jesus. It has little to do with becoming one with the life of the suffering servant, of accepting the paradoxical logic of Jesus' life as the inner structure of one's own. Instead, baptism is regarded by many as something we are supposed to do for little children, as illustrated by the nervous mother who telephoned her minister saying: "Father, I want to have my kid done. Is it O.K.?"

Unfortunately when baptism is seen this way, confirmation, the second act in the initiation drama, has nothing on which to build. Who can confirm a baptismal vow that has no substance? Who can "complete" a life-long process that has lost its contact with life?

And if baptism and confirmation lose their meaning, the first communion is without significance. The church has lost its saltiness. And the society suffers from an anemic condition that can be blamed, in part, on the church's inability to celebrate its faith with integrity.

Baptism: The Foundation of Christian Initiation

This need not be the case. The church has a rich heritage of role models, archetypal images, doctrines, and rituals that are waiting to be re-formed into a powerful rite of passage to Christian adulthood. This new rite should certainly include confirmation. It should also allow for human transformation of the magnitude of the "conversion experience." But the foundation should be the sacrament of baptism, which is the heart of the Christian rite of initiation into the community of faith.

Paul's Use of Classical Images of Initiation

The first attempt to explain the meaning of baptism comes from Paul, who relies heavily on the classic motifs of initiation. In the letter to the Galatians he speaks of baptism as the rite by which Christians are grafted into the body of Christ, where their new unity obscures all previous divisions of humankind, and the believer is given a taste of the universal quality of existence:

> Baptized into union with him, you have put on Christ as a garment. There is no such thing as Jew or Greek, slave and free, male and female; for you are all one person in Christ Jesus (Galatians 3:27–28 NEB).

In the first letter to the Corinthians Paul compares baptism to the passage of the Israelites from bondage to freedom.

> You should understand, my brothers, that our ancestors were all under a pillar of a cloud, and all of them passed through the Red Sea; and so they all received baptism into the fellowship of Moses in cloud and sea. They all ate the supernatural food, and drank the same supernatural drink; I mean, they all drank from the supernatural rock that accompanied their travels—the rock was Christ (1 Corinthians 10:1–3 NEB).

In two of his most explicit sections on baptism, Paul explains the rite in terms of the movement from death to birth in Jesus Christ.

> Do you not know that all of us who have been baptized into Christ Jesus were baptized into his death? We were buried therefore with him by baptism into death, so that as Christ was raised from the dead by the glory of the Father, we too might walk in newness of life.

69

For if we have been united with him in a death like his, we shall certainly be united with him in a resurrection like his. We know that our old self was crucified with him so that the sinful body might be destroyed, and we might no longer be enslaved to sin. For he who has died is freed from sin. But if we have died with Christ, we believe that we shall also live with him (Romans 6:3–8).

In Christ also you were circumcised, not in a physical sense, but by being divested of the lower nature; this is Christ's way of circumcision. For in baptism you were buried with him, in baptism also you were raised to life with him through your faith in the active power of God, who raised you from the dead. And although you were dead because of your sins and because you were morally uncircumcised, he has made you alive in Christ (Colossians 2:11–13 NEB).

By now the reader should be aware of the many references to classic initiation themes. But there is one new quality in Paul's explanation: the idea that we who are baptized "put on Christ as a garment," "become one person in Christ Jesus," "are incorporated in his death and are made one with him in resurrection like his," and are "alive in Christ." Somehow, through the initiation rite of baptism, we are made Christians; we are incorporated into the life of Christ.

Exactly how this happens we will never know. Not only does the mystery defy understanding, but the rituals that express the mystery are themselves lost in mystery. Yet we must try to uncover the history of the sacrament of baptism from the first century to the twentieth.

This is very tricky business. Our sources are few and sadly limited in what they tell us. We have no reliable record of worship practices during the time of Jesus' earthly life or in the period of the early church. The scriptures were not meant to serve as a book of worship. At best we get hints. At worst we get misled.

The task is complicated by the intricate creative process by which liturgies are brought to life. They are composed, which means that any written records are meant to be performed, not merely read. But there is still more to confuse our task. Unlike the composers of music, those who create liturgies "are not individuals but whole peoples, and the composition evolves so slowly as a rule that the process is rarely remarked upon even by those who know best."[8] This is particularly true of a ritual like baptism, which makes use of one of the universal symbols of regeneration, immersion in water. Baptism, in a multiplicity of forms, has been practiced by peoples all over this earth. Throughout the twenty centuries of Christian baptism, the rite "has always been a compound act absorbing cultural patterns into itself: it has taken on definite shape in various cultures, shaping those cultures in return."[9]

Practices of the New Testament Church

The cultures that influenced first century baptism were the Greco-Roman world and Judaism. The most significant contribution of the former was the custom of public bathing. Even now, visitors to Europe find ruins of Roman baths next to the arenas, amphitheaters, and forums. Centuries ago, those baths were the center of the community's social life, providing much more than an opportunity to get clean.

> While one obviously could wash without bathing as one could eat without dining, both took on vastly enriched social and personal importance. . . . which the modern world is only beginning to recover.[10]

The impact of Judaism was more directly related to baptism itself. As has been said, there was no puberty rite in Judaism during the time of Jesus. Circumcision was for infants. The Bar Mitzvah entered the liturgical picture in the fourteenth century. There was, nevertheless, a form of baptism. When a person chose to convert to Judaism, the convert was required to prepare by studying the Torah. At the conclusion of the preparation, males were circumcised and both male and

71

female were baptized. The baptism was envisioned as a means of washing away the impurities of the Gentile world and receiving the converts into the covenant community. While they were immersed in water, sections of the Torah were read over them.

The rabbis interpreted the meaning of the baptism in terms of initiation.

> One who separates himself from uncircumcision is like one who is separated from the grave. One who becomes a proselyte is like one newly born.[11]

John the Baptist made use of the culture's knowledge of the baptismal motif in his call to repentance. Standing in the flowing waters of the Jordan River he cried, "Repent, for the kingdom of God is at hand" (Matthew 3:2). People, apparently Jew and Gentile alike, heard John's call, were baptized, and began wondering if he might actually be the long-awaited Messiah. John answered, "I baptize you with water for repentance, but . . . he will baptize you with the Holy Spirit and with fire" (Matthew 3:11).

Jesus, as we know, was baptized. We do not know, however, if he baptized others. It is generally assumed that he did not baptize in water, as did the rabbis or John. But we believe he did baptize with the spirit, thereby radically changing the lives he touched, creating both a new community and a new ethic. When he asked the disciples, "Can you be baptized with the baptism with which I am baptized?" he did not expect them to return to the Jordan for some ritual re-enactment of his immersion in the water. Rather he was inquiring about their capacity to undergo the trials of their life of service.

The stories of the earliest Christians are filled with accounts of their "being baptized with the baptism with which he was baptized." They were baptized in the Spirit. They created a new community of faith; they attempted to live by a radical ethic of Christian love. And they were persecuted.

But their stories do not tell us whether they were baptized in any other sense of the word. Were they immersed in water? Were they even touched by water? Was baptism limited to adults? If a whole household was baptized, did that necessarily include children? Throughout the ages, men and women of good will have differed in their answers to these questions. The differences are possible because the scriptures are neither definitive nor descriptive in discussing the ritual of Christian baptism.

The Didache

The first known attempt to be definitive is found in the *Didache,* a set of teachings for the church, which some date as early as A.D. 100. It tersely instructs as follows:

> Now about baptism: this is how to baptize. Give public instruction on all these points, and then "baptize" in running water, "in the name of the Father and of the Son and of the Holy Spirit." If you do not have running water, baptize in some other. If you cannot in cold, then in warm. If you have neither, then pour water on the head three times "in the name of the Father, Son, and Holy Spirit." Before the baptism, moreover, the one who baptizes and the one being baptized must fast, and any others who can. And you must tell the one being baptized to fast for one or two days beforehand.[12]

The Apostolic Tradition of Hippolytus

Several other reports on baptismal practices from the early church report elaboration on this most primitive statement from the *Didache,* but the fullest account from the early church comes from the apostolic tradition associated with the name of Hippolytus, a leader of the church in the beginning of the third century. The document begins by stating its purpose.

> We have set down those things which are worthy of note about the gifts which God has bestowed on man . . . And now, led on by the love for all the saints, we have proceeded to the summit of the tradition which befits the churches, in order that

those who have been taught by our exposition may guard that tradition.[19]

Of the traditions surrounding baptism as initiation into the Christian community, they speak with remarkable specificity. The initiation begins, as all classic initiations begin, with an act separating the candidate from his or her former life. The initiation then proceeds to a period of learning and concludes with an act of culmination and incorporation.

The Rite of Separation   The explanation of the act of separation reads as follows:

OF NEWCOMERS TO THE FAITH

Those who come forward for the first time to hear the word shall first be brought to the teachers before all the people arrive, and shall be questioned about their reason for coming to the faith. And those who have brought them shall bear witness about them, whether they are capable of hearing the word. They shall be questioned about their state of life: has he a wife? Is he the slave of a believer? Does his master allow him? Let him hear the word. If his master does not bear witness about him that he is a good man, he shall be rejected. If his master is a heathen, teach him to please his master, that there be no scandal. If any man has a wife, or a woman a husband, they shall be taught to be contented, the man with his wife and the woman with her husband. But if any man is not living with a wife, he shall be instructed not to fornicate, but to take a wife lawfully or remain as he is. If anyone is possessed by a demon, he shall not hear the word of teaching until he is pure.

OF CRAFTS AND PROFESSIONS

Inquiry shall be made about the crafts and professions of those who are brought for instruction. If a man is a brothel-keeper, let him cease or be rejected. If anyone is a sculptor or a painter, let them be instructed not to make idols; let them cease or be rejected. If anyone is an actor or gives theatrical performances, let him cease or be rejected. He who teaches children had best cease.[14]

The list of crafts and professions that must be stopped goes on and on. If he is a charioteer who competes in the games, or goes to them, let him cease or be rejected. A gladiator, a teacher of gladiators, a public official employed in gladiatorial business, a priest, a keeper of idols, a soldier who kills, a magistrate "who wears purple," a prostitute, a profligate, or a eunuch, a charmer, and so on. When the list seems to have exhausted itself, there is one final note. "If we have left anything out, the facts themselves will teach you; for we all have the Spirit of God."[15] Those who are concerned to protect the tradition have thereby covered themselves. Newcomers to the faith must separate themselves from all in their former life that is unacceptable to God—or be rejected.

The Journey into Understanding The second stage of initiation into the Christian community, generally the stage of learning "the techniques and mysteries" of the new life, is called "The Time of Hearing the Word." The information about this stage is limited. "Catechumens shall continue to hear the word for three years. But if a man is keen, and perseveres well in the matter, the time shall not be judged, but only his conduct."[16]

There is another comment about the candidate during the time of his catechumenate:

> If a catechumen is arrested for the name of the Lord, let him not be in two minds about his witness. For if he suffers violence and is killed (before he has received baptism) for the forgiveness of his sins, he will be justified, for he has received baptism in his blood.[17]

The Rite of Incorporation The third stage of the initiation is the richest and receives the fullest treatment by the writer of the *Apostolic Tradition*. It takes little imagination to appreciate the awesomeness of the experience of baptism as it must have been performed in the third century.

As the three years are ending and the teacher finishes giving instructions, "let the catechumens pray by themselves, still separated from the faithful . . . let their lives be examined . . . let hands be laid on them daily while they are exorcised."[18] They shall be instructed to bathe on Thursday, to fast on Friday, and to keep vigil on Saturday. Then comes the day of their birth.

OF THE CONFERRING OF HOLY BAPTISM

At the time when the cock crows, first let prayer be made over the water. Let the water be flowing in the font or poured over it. Let it be thus unless there is some necessity; if the necessity is permanent and urgent, use what water you can find. They shall take off their clothes. Baptize the little ones first. All those who cannot speak for themselves, their parents or someone from their family shall speak for them. Then baptize the men, and lastly the women, who shall have loosened all their hair, and laid down the gold and silver ornaments which they have on them. Let no one take any alien object down into the water. And at the time fixed for baptizing, the bishop shall give thanks over the oil, which he puts in a vessel: one calls it 'oil of exorcism.' And a deacon takes the oil of exorcism and stands on the priest's left; and another deacon takes the oil of thanksgiving and stands on the priest's right. And when the priest takes each one of those who are to receive baptism, he shall bid him renounce, saying:

I renounce you, Satan, and all your service and all your works.

And when each one has renounced all this, he shall anoint him with the oil of exorcism, saying to him:

Let every spirit depart far from you.

And in this way he shall hand him over naked to the bishop or the priest who stands by the water to baptize. In the same way a deacon shall descend with him into the water and say, helping him to say:

I believe in one God, the Father almighty . . .

And then, when he has come up, he shall be anointed from the oil of thanksgiving by the presbyter, who says:

I anoint you with holy oil in the name of Jesus Christ.

And so each of them shall wipe himself and put on his clothes, and then he shall enter into the church.[19]

Once in the church they are greeted by the faithful and invited to share the meal. First the bread. Then three cups: a cup of water, a cup of milk and honey, and a cup of wine.

The initiation to the Christian faith as practiced in the third century has obvious power. There is no way to know when the tradition preserved by Hippolytus first came to be used. It is unlikely that a ritual this powerful and elaborate would go unmentioned by those who told the story of the early church in scripture; therefore, we cannot claim that this form of baptism is scriptural. On the other hand, it can be rightly argued that all the components of this third century baptismal rite are inspired by the scriptures.

The act of separation from one's former life is demanded by John the Baptist, and repeated by Jesus in his insistent call to the disciples to leave their nets, to leave "house or wife or brothers or parents or children, for the sake of the kingdom of God" (Luke 18:29). The apostles pick up the theme with Peter's Pentecost sermon. "Each one of you must turn away from your sins and be baptized" (Acts 2:38 TEV).

The second act of the initiation is the period of learning the mysteries and techniques of the new way. Again the scriptures abound with examples: the forty years in the wilderness for the People of Israel, the forty days of the temptation for Jesus of Nazareth, the three years of discipleship for the apostles, the three days of blindness suffered by Paul, during which he did not eat or drink, and after which Ananias laid hands on him. "And immediately something like scales fell from his eyes and he regained his sight. Then he rose and was baptized, and took food and was strengthened" (Acts 9:18).

The progression in Paul's experience involves a movement from the second to the third stage of initiation. Even in this brief passage we see several of the practices of the third century baptism: the laying of hands, the baptism—but not necessarily a water baptism—and the meal at the end of the ordeal. The other custom that plays such an important part in the initiation of Hippolytus, namely the anointing with oil, is also alluded to in scripture, even though it is nowhere described or prescribed. Jesus is anointed "to preach good news to the poor" (Luke 4:18). John speaks of our "having an anointing from the Holy One, whereby we know all things." (1 John 2:20 K). And Paul says, "It is God who establishes us with you in Christ [*Christon*] and has anointed us [*Chrisas*]" (2 Corinthians 1:21 K). The name Christ is not the family name of Jesus of Nazareth. Christ is the Greek word for Messiah, which is the Hebrew word for the Anointed One. The phenomenon of anointing is tied to the very center of our faith.

Thus, by the third century there existed a tradition of initiation that needed to be guarded lest it be compromised. We cannot say when and where the tradition first arose. Surely it was practiced in the second century, possibly in the first.

The initiation experience has the three primary movements of all rites of passage—separation, transition, incorporation. Furthermore it includes numerous motifs common to initiation rites. In brief, the rite of initiation practiced by the Christian church in the third century was "the real thing!" This raises the question: What happened to it?

Dismembering Christian Initiation

It appears that the shape and meaning of the initiation rites remained reasonably constant for several centuries. But gradually, erosion set in that led to the separation of confirmation from baptism.

The Roman Tradition

The first sign of any breakup was a minor one. The confirmation part of the ritual was put at the end of the service, after the eucharist. From that followed another change, also seemingly minor. The confirmation part of the service was pushed back a week and celebrated at the end of

78

the Easter octave. Then came a logistical concern. As the church grew and its life became more complex, it became difficult for a bishop to be present at all baptisms. To accommodate this scheduling problem it was decided that local priests could baptize, while the anointing of confirmation was reserved for the visiting bishop. By now the tendency to separate baptism from confirmation had its own momentum. By the ninth century these two parts of Christian initiation were separated by years.

Since confirmation now stood alone, no longer buttressed by baptism immediately preceding it or first communion immediately following it, the rite needed its own theological support system. It was given one, primarily through the writing of Thomas Aquinas. Before Thomas, scholars had cited Old Testament anointings—especially that of King David—to justify those parts of the old initiation now included in the isolated rite of confirmation. As long as confirmation was clearly connected to baptism, no additional justification was needed. But once separated and labeled as "the sacrament of the fullness of grace," Thomas reasoned that it must be founded on something more than Old Testament precedents. It must be rooted in the very life and ministry of Christ himself. Thomas Aquinas cited Pope Melchides, Pope Eusebius, and Pope Urban, in support of the proposition that confirmation was a sacramental prerequisite for "the fullness of grace." Only with confirmation could one complete the process begun with baptism. The powers given at baptism were sufficient for childhood, but in order to be a full-fledged Christian one also must be confirmed. Confirmation gives the power necessary for "spiritual adulthood."[20]

The influence of Thomas Aquinas was so great that this understanding was accepted as the official position of the Roman church, and the liturgical practices surrounding initiation remained fixed for centuries. The most significant change since the Middle Ages in Roman liturgies regarding initiation did not occur until the twentieth century. In 1910 Pope Pius X, as part of an effort to encourage more frequent attendance at the eucharist, lowered the age of first communion from adolescence to "the dawn of the use of reason" in early childhood.[21]

There was widespread resistance to the change. It is interesting to note that the arguments were almost always couched in terms of religious education. The devout wondered whether children could really understand—or how best to teach such an inscrutable mystery. No one seemed concerned about the further dissolution of an initiation rite. By the beginning of the twentieth century, most Catholics barely realized that they had an initiation rite. It had been fractured long ago. Its components were strewn all over the years of childhood. Baptism came as soon after birth as feasible. Confirmation came with adolescence. First communion came somewhere in between. And catechizing was taken over by the religious educators; no longer was the teaching about the faith directly related to initiation.

The Eastern Church

We have followed, though somewhat cursorily, the path the Roman Catholic church has taken regarding initiation from the first century to the twentieth. Another major route is that followed by the Eastern Church, which can be summarized in a few words. Orthodox Christianity has retained much of the basic initiation rite of the third century. A decision was made to allow local priests to baptize and to anoint, using oil blessed by the bishop. Consequently, to this day baptism, consignation, confirmation, and first communion are contained in a single liturgical event. This event is not, however, preceded by catechizing, since Orthodox initiation customarily occurs in infancy.

The Reformation Churches

The great dividing of the ways in the Western church that occurred during the Reformation brought considerable debate about sacraments and rites, including baptism, confirmation, first communion and catechizing. But rarely did the debate speak directly to initiation experience as a whole. The controversies centered on two other issues: (1) the meaning and number of the sacraments, and (2) the appropriate age for baptism.

On the first issue, three paths were followed. The Anglicans affirmed the Roman Catholic doctrine, listing seven sacraments: baptism, communion, penance, confirmation, marriage, ordination, and last rites. Luther, Calvin, and the reformers nearest the theological center of the Reformation argued that there were but two sacraments: baptism and communion. The more radical reformers reasoned that since all life was a sacrament, no particular liturgical acts should be set apart as sacraments.

On the second issue—the appropriate age for baptism— two distinct paths were pursued. Some said it was appropriate to baptize infants, as was apparently the tradition of the church since the time of Christ. Others claimed that baptism should be reserved for those with sufficient maturity to take responsibility for their faith decisions. Those two divergent positions are well known, as is the history of prejudice and persecution resulting from the divergence.

What may not be known is that many of the most thoughtful Reformation theologians have seen the wisdom of both ways and have sought to reconcile the differences. Huldreich Zwingli, a German-Swiss theologian, reasoned that baptism is similar to circumcision, that a child of at least one Christian parent is holy, and that the baptism of infants is, consequently, acceptable but not necessary. The New Testament, he argued, neither commends nor prohibits the baptism of infants.

John Calvin, the Reformer of Geneva, follows a similar line of reasoning:

> The offspring of believers are born holy, because their children, while still in the womb, before they breathe the vital

air, are included in the covenant of eternal life . . . Now, then, when they make baptism to be so necessary that they exclude all who have not been dipped with it from the hope of salvation, they both insult God and also involve themselves in great absurdity.[22]

To Calvin:

Baptism is the sign of the initiation by which we are received into the society of the church, in order that, engrafted in Christ, we may be reckoned among God's children . . . the chief point of baptism (is) to receive baptism with this promise: 'He who believes and is baptized is saved.'" (Mark 16:16)[23]

The ordinary arrangement requires belief before baptism. But with children, Calvin argues for a reversal of the order.

Infants are baptized unto future repentance and faith, and even though these have not yet been formed in them, the seed of both lies hidden within them by the secret workings of the Spirit.[24]

Re-membering Christian Initiation

For four centuries, the several traditions of the Reformation pursued their separate ways, generating boundless energy on the divisive question of infant versus believers' baptism, but directing precious little attention to the deeper issue of initiation. There was some concern for confirmation, which was generally seen more as an educational opportunity than an act of liturgical significance. Consequently, confirmation has remained in Protestantism what it was in Catholicism—an undeveloped rite.

Brunner and Barth

Not until the beginning of this century was the issue of initiation addressed. The first to speak was the Swiss theologian Emil Brunner. In 1937, he began to talk about "the primitive wholeness of Christian initiation" and yearned

82

for a return "to the primitive practice" by which children were enrolled as catechumens until they were baptized, confirmed, and invited to the Lord's table in one service.[25]

A few years later, Karl Barth raised his mighty voice on the same matter. In a book on *The Teaching of the Church Regarding Baptism,* Barth uses the classic imagery of initiation. Baptism is a rite of death and resurrection, or to be exact:

> The threat of death and the deliverance to life, in the midst of which (the baptizand) is concerned to no one but himself as the one who is threatened and delivered; in which also he is not only dealt with but, by yielding himself to this threat of deliverance finds himself taking an active part.[26]

> What happens to a man in baptism is that he is placed and places himself in the darkness and the light of this fact: that in the death and resurrection of Jesus Christ he also is dead and risen again.[27]

Then Karl Barth drops his real bombshell:

> Baptism without the willingness and readiness to be baptized is true, effectual, and effective baptism, but it is not correct; it is not done in obedience, it is not administered according to the proper order and therefore is necessarily a clouded baptism. It must and ought not be repeated. It is, however, a wound in the body of the Church and a weakness for the baptized, which certainly can be cured but which are so dangerous that another question presents itself to the Church: how long is she prepared to be guilty of the occasioning of this wounding and weakening through the baptismal practice which is, from this standpoint, arbitrary and despotic?[28]

It is impossible to know if Karl Barth's writing contributed to the subsequent shift in the church's understanding and practice of initiation, or simply anticipated it. In any case, there has been a gradual movement in the last several decades back to what Emil Brunner called "the primitive wholeness of Christian invitation."

The Second Vatican Council and Roman Reform

Perhaps the most significant change came as a result of the Second Vatican Council convened by Pope John XXIII. Baptismal reform has been called "the sleeper" among the sacramental and liturgical issues, for although the mass was discussed at length and radically modified, the consideration of baptism was relegated to Council commissions, which not only reviewed baptism but recommended "the complete overhaul of Catholic initiatory practice." The commission's recommendations came in three separate documents. The first was on the baptism of children (1969); the second, on confirmation (1971); the last and most comprehensive, on the initiation of adults (1972). The effect of all three was to call the Roman Catholic church and perhaps the whole catholic church to rediscover its lost rite.

The response to the call has been less than overwhelming. Only one half of the dioceses in this country bothered to return a questionnaire from the Bishop's Commission on the Liturgy concerning implementation of the Rite of Christian Initiation of Adults. Of those who returned it, only less than one half indicated some work on adult initiation; of those, less than one half expressed interest in being part of a national study. "As one commentator suggested, "this is probably more than sloth." This is a major overhaul of Catholic worship customs. "We just don't know where to begin translating this vision into practice."[29]

Other Liturgical Churches

But even though the movement toward adult initiation is small at this time, it is gaining momentum and picking up adherents from different areas of the church. At one end of the spectrum, two of the more liturgical traditions—Lutheran and Episcopal—have raised questions about initiation as a result of revision to their worship books. The Episcopalians have gone beyond the initial revisions in the publication of several Prayer Book studies. The studies acknowledge that "sacramental practice usually alters very slowly," but that it nevertheless must come.

> Thus, those who suggest that a change in sacramental practice is indicative of a change in understanding of the faith are correct in their assertion—not that there is a deliberate attempt to undermine "the teaching of the Church," but rather that there has already been a gradual and serious change in the Church's frame of reference (usually in the total sense of its religious and cultural self awareness), and that suddenly it is recognized that the context in which Christian faith and practice are understood is no longer what it was.[30]

The purpose of the recent change is the unification of "the rites of Christian Initiation so that it would be quite clear in the Church's liturgical celebration that there is only one fundamental ritual expression of Initiation." Baptism is the foundation of this unified Initiation Rite. And adults are named as the "normative candidates."[31] "The structure of the new rite is significant: adults and older children are presented first. The rite itself thus conveys the fact that Baptism implies an adult or mature commitment to Jesus Christ.[32] The authors of the study wisely concede "the Baptism of infants is in no sense likely to disappear, but (there is an) emergence of greater numbers of adult candidates."[33]

The Free Churches
If these liturgical churches represent one end of the spectrum, the free church tradition represents the other. And there, in addition to our initiation in a Congregational church in Middletown, Connecticut, we find isolated examples of other local churches rediscovering the need to initiate their young people into Christian adulthood. A Black church in the Philadelphia area has created an initiation called Orita. The term originates with the Yoruba tribe in West Africa and means "crossroads." The purpose of the ritual is to impress upon the initiates their

responsibility for their moral conduct from a Christian perspective . . . This Orita Ceremony is designed to help prepare the pilgrim not just for the parish, but for the world. Whenever the pilgrim goes, he or she can never forget that the religious community, along with one's immediate family, come together in the ceremony and recognized his or her efforts to find life's meaning. It should be the purpose of the religious community to send forth a religious person—not just a good personality—into the world with a good character nurtured in the Christian faith.[34]

Orita requirements take the pilgrims through a variety of challenges on such matters as managing the family budget, exploring career and educational opportunities, reliving Black history, studying the Bible, and finally presenting "the Orita speech" to the congregation.

There are also reports from Christian congregations in Africa that have recreated a learning experience and ritual to pass on their tradition as they prepare emerging adults for the ever-changing world. "We get away from the schoolroom. We are not learning a lesson, but learning to live."[34] The final ritual serves as a reminder of the power of initiation symbols.

During the paschal vigil, the symbolism of death and resurrection is intensely expressed. Baptism is conferred in a sort of hollow tomb dug in the ground, or in a baptismal pool filled with water to thigh level.[36]

The Future of Christian Initiation: The Growing Urgency

It is encouraging to hear reports of the church finding the power of this symbolism, for in a day when both confirmation and baptism are being ignored by Christians, there is a growing concern that some form of non-Christian water baptism might appear. The question is whether the "new" water baptism will serve or disserve the world.

The power of these archetypal images is too great to be rendered null and void by any process of deliberate exclusion.

If they are not sanctified within the Christian context, they will most certainly present themselves in demonic forms. To find a way of allowing Baptism to exercise its power within the Christian community at the deepest level of the human psyche is one of the most urgent tasks of our day.[37]

This urgency is echoed by a Roman Catholic liturgical scholar. The rediscovery of our lost rite of initiation is crucial:

Its ramifications are so multitudinous as to suggest that the sequence sustained through the year and reaching its peak in the annual rhythms of Lent and the celebration of Easter, constitutes the church's radical business for the good of the world itself.[38]

Still another voice expresses the challenge.

Today we find ourselves caught with our hands full of unfinished business. Ours is a humpty dumpty problem: all the king's horses and all the king's men have not yet succeeded in putting back together the fractured rite of Christian initiation. That task is likely to continue to challenge us in the years ahead.[39]

Three Issues

We move to the years ahead with the sense that paths are converging and Christians all over the earth are coming to see the need for a unified and powerful rite of Christian initiation. As we move into the future it is important that we be aware of the issues that have disrupted Christian unity and taken us on divergent paths: the slow pace of liturgical change, the dangers in symbolic expression, and the debate over the age of baptism.

First, do not be discouraged by the slow pace of liturgical change; remember that liturgies are not "composed" by individuals, but by peoples; they take lifetimes to create. Second, beware of the Scylla and Charybdis of symbolic expression; if there is too little, the deepest levels of the psyche will not be touched; if there is too much, the psyche will not be able to process it. Third, take seriously the debate about the appropriate age of baptism; it has divided the church through the ages; it has consistently thrown the church off the track in the search for our lost rite of initiation.

The first two concerns will be dealt with throughout this book. The third deserves specific comment at this time.

The Age of Baptism

It almost seems a truism that if there are two sides of an argument and one is right, then the other must be wrong. The acceptance of this line of reasoning has caused untold hardship and persecution throughout the history of the church. This is tragic, especially as it relates to baptism and initiation, because a deeper truth is that right may exist on both sides of the argument. And an even deeper truth is that there may be ways to resolve an argument that do not violate either side.

Infants apparently have been baptized along with adults since the days of the apostles. The scriptures tell of converts who were baptized "along with their households," which would seem to include both slaves and children. An early church letter from John the Deacon reports,

> I must say plainly and at once, in case I seemed to have overlooked the point, that all these things are done even to infants, who by reason of their youth understood nothing.[40]

In the initiation service at the time of Hippolytus, the record shows that children were baptized, even though the three-year catechumenate and the elaborate renunciation of a former life imply that the initiation was meant for adults.

> Baptize the little ones first. All those who can speak for themselves shall do so. As for those who cannot speak for themselves, their parents or someone from the family shall speak for them.[41]

Remember also that John Calvin, whose writings represent the epitome of systematic theology during the Reformation, made room for both believers' baptism and infant baptism.

The ordinary arrangement required belief before baptism, but infants may be "baptized unto future repentance and faith, and even though they have not yet been formed in them, the seed of both lies hidden within them by the secret workings of the Spirit."[42]

A Norm for Baptism

Calvin gives us the clue to resolving the problem. The full resolution is expounded by a Roman Catholic theologian. Commenting upon *The Rites of Christian Initiation of Adults,* Father Aiden Kavanagh introduces us to the concept of "the norm."

> A norm . . . has nothing to do with the number of times a thing is done, but it has everything to do with the standard according to which a thing is done. So long as the norm is in place both in practice and in the awareness of those who are engaged in it, the situation is capable of being judged "normal" even though the norm must be departed from to some extent, even frequently, due to the exigencies of time, place, pastoral considerations, physical inabilities, or whatever.[43]

With this definition of a norm in mind, Father Kavanagh sets forth the norm of Christian baptism.

> Baptism is the solemn sacramental initiation done especially at the paschal vigil and preceded by a catechumenate of serious content and considerable duration. This implies strongly, even if it does not require, that the (candidate) be an adult or at least a child well advanced in years.[44]

A Norm for Christian Initiation

Expanding ever so slightly on this statement, we can suggest a norm of Christian initiation. Initiation is the process by which persons are (1) separated from the world of childhood, (2) subjected to a period of training and testing during which they are exposed to the techniques and mysteries of Christian adulthood, and (3) received into the Christian community with appropriate rituals. The appropriate ritual of incorporation should include:

- Baptism or vicarious baptism.
- Confirmation, with any of several liturgical acts: laying on of hands, signing with the cross, anointing, commissioning, extending the right hand of fellowship, owning the covenant.
- A meal of bread and wine.

Such a norm assumes the initiate to be an adolescent or adult.

That is the proposed norm of Christian initiation. Actual initiations of necessity would vary from this norm at any number of points. With this norm in mind, however, the Christian church can offer its services to the turbulent world of adolescence. It can contribute something of great value, something that is now missing in our society: a renewed rite of passage to adulthood: Christian initiation.

Part Two

CHAPTER FIVE

The Wilderness of Adolescence

When Paul wrote his letter to the church in Ephesus, he spoke with considerable wisdom about the process of growing up.

> So shall we at last attain to the unity inherent in our faith and our knowledge of the Son of God—to mature manhood, measured by nothing less than the full stature of Christ. We are no longer to be children, tossed by the waves and whirled about by every fresh gust of teaching, dupes of crafty rogues and their deceitful schemes. No, let us speak the truth in love; so shall we fully grow up into Christ (Ephesians 4:13–15 NEB).

As I look out on our society, I am shocked at how many persons, young and old, have been duped by the "crafty rogues," tossed by the waves and whirled about by fresh gusts of teaching which blow relentlessly upon us, trying to convince us that the way to fulfillment is changing and we must change with it. I see innumerable adolescents twisted about by this confusing state of affairs. And I see many adults still living out their adolescence.

Adolescence and Adulthood

Part of the reason for this is that we fail to appreciate the interrelatedness of adulthood and adolescence. I have long been persuaded that the words we use control our lives—often in ways that we fail to understand. In order to increase our control and our understanding of our lives, then, it is often valuable to trace the words we use back to their origins.

When I looked at the words, "adult" and "adolescent," I suspected that they must be related in some integral way. When I checked an etymological dictionary, my suspicions were confirmed. Both words have the same Latin root, *adolescere,* which means "to grow up." Adolescent comes from the present participle; adult from the past participle. An adolescent is, literally, "one growing up;" an adult is "one grown up." The adolescent and the adult derive their being from each other. Adults provide the meaning and shape of adolescence. They live out the "state of grown-upness" into which adolescents will grow.

For the children in a primitive culture, there was a well-defined adulthood into which they could mature. That state of maturity was given definition by the stories of the tribal heroes and the rite of initiation. But for the modern adolescent, there is very little clarity about adulthood. There is no clear statement of the goal to which one aspires. And, as has been pointed out, there are only vestigial rituals of initiation, scattered indiscriminately over a series of years.

The most perceptive students of adolescence bemoan this uncertainty:

> The adolescent of today is exposed to an unusually large number of people who have no consistently formulated value system. Few people are intensely dedicated to anything, and often those who are, are as erratically fanatical in their dedication as the adolescent in his confusion is apt to be. The church, a philosophy, the nation as a focus for patriotism, these and other areas which in the past many believed in with emotional conviction—are not a viable part of the thoughts and lives of large groups of people today. This may make it more difficult for the adolescent to find a framework for himself.[1]

This (maturing) process may be frustrated and emptied of meaning in a society which, like our own, is hostile to clarity and vividness. Our culture impedes the clear definition of any faithful self image—indeed, of any clear image whatsoever. We do not break images; there are few iconoclasts among us. Instead, we blur and soften them. The resulting pliability gives life in our society its familiar, plastic texture. It also makes adolescence more difficult, more dangerous, and more troublesome to the adolescent and to society itself. And it makes adolescence rarer.[2]

There are many ways to explain this lack of clarity in our society. The church, in responding to the secularism and pluralism of our age, has compromised its eternal task of raising up the heroes from the past and the heroic possibilities for the future. More specifically, the church has defaulted on its fundamental task of presenting Jesus Christ, the "Man for Others," as the model of mature adulthood.

But to focus only on the church is to miss the full range of our present confusion. The dynamics of our society, together with the psycho-sexual dynamics of adolescence, conspire to confound clarity and perpetuate perplexity.

Lost in the Wilderness

One of the most striking features of our society, when viewed from the perspective of an emerging adolescent, is that there is no single moment when a person can claim to have arrived at adulthood. In fact, there is no single moment when one can claim to have even started on the journey toward adulthood. There is rather a frightening disarray of non-events, both public and private, that stretch out over a decade.

Partial Initiations—Private and Public

The private events are encountered first. Generally, by age twelve or thirteen—but sometimes as early as nine or ten—girls experience menarche, first menstruation. With the onset of menstruation, the secondary sex characteristics develop. The breasts grow, the body becomes more shapely, pubic hair gradually appears, and frequently there is a dramatic spurt of growth. Between ages nine and twelve, in response to these mystifying changes, girls—young women—become deeply concerned about how they look. They suffer the often embarrassing experience of purchasing their first brassiere and experimenting with cosmetics.

Boys have no point of demarcation as precise as menarche. Their bodies grow and assume a more masculine shape in a barely discernable process. They grow pubic, body, and facial hair. And they gain height, albeit somewhat later than they had hoped. Boys usually do not experience the growth spurt until twelve to fifteen, which means that during early adolescence most girls will be taller than most boys, a fact which is aggravated by the societal norm somehow telling even young men that they are supposed to be tall, dark, and handsome. The closest parallel to menstruation is ejaculation, most often occurring first as mysterious "nocturnal emissions" during the early teenage years. The closest parallel to the purchase of the brassiere is the purchase of the jock. Comparable to the use of cosmetics is the use of the razor, accompanied by the tell-tale nicks under the chin.

Anyone experiencing or remembering the events of early puberty knows how lonely these private encounters with adulthood can be—or how crushed one feels when the first attempts to communicate one's new state of being to the public fail to go smoothly. I have heard numerous tales—horror tales—about clerks behind the intimate apparel counter or smark alecks in the sporting goods department who questioned: "Do you need to spend your parents' money on that!" I have heard painful accounts of crooked lipstick and missed peach fuzz and—God forbid—soiled sheets.

Furthermore, I have heard story after story about the awkwardness of early dating: How clumsy one feels when asking for a date. How unprepared for that first invitation.

How easy it is to say yes when one really means no—to say no when one really means yes! How absolutely impossible it is to know what one means or wants!

Most parents don't help much in these earliest stages of puberty. They seem to have such a deep-seated ambivalence about their children's maturing that all their efforts to understand are undermined by an occasional overheard chuckle about the latest embarrassment. Similarly, many age mates cannot help to ease the loneliness, because one can never be sure what is happening in their lives. The doubt is always there: "Maybe I'm the only one going through this agony!"

So lonely is the encounter with these first private experiences with emerging sexuality and emerging selfhood, that most adolescents yearn for the public events that will at least mark the growth process. Of those few young people who turn to the church for confirmation, it appears that the primary motivating factor is not a desire to confirm a belief system, but a need to be recognized as adults and accepted into some legitimate adult community.

But confirmation pales into insignificance when compared to what most adolescents identify as the key moment of passage to adulthood. The sixteenth birthday generally brings with it the opportunity to get one's driver's license. The moment when that license is granted by some anonymous bureaucrat, the adolescent, as much as any other time, becomes an adult. The license brings with it authority, status, flexibility, freedom, an unprecedented capacity to move, to speed, to show off, to have privacy, to injure, and even to kill.

Society offers several other turning points in the way of adulthood. Graduation is the exit rite from the institution of adolescence, the high school. The eighteenth birthday is generally recognized as the point in life when one can legally vote, drink, gamble, join the service, go to any movie without parental permission. Commencement from college, the awarding of the graduate degree, marriage, the first full-time job, the first pay check, the first baby . . . all are times at which individuals and the society mark the passage to adulthood.

Self-Initiations

In addition to these, there is another long list of experiences not legitimized by society. In our culture, street initiations and self-initiations abound. Elementary school students smoke and drink in order to "feel big." High schools are constantly combatting abuse of alcohol and drugs. About ten percent of all teenage girls—one million in all—become pregnant each year. About 600,000 give birth each year, and the greatest increase is in girls under 14![3] Teenage crime, teenage suicide, teenage runaways, teenage despair and confusion are on the rise everywhere.

One self-initiated youngster wrote about her initiation:

I couldn't tell what was happening to me. My heart was gone and my body languished. I did not want it to be so, but my body was inert and defenseless. I resisted mentally but my body floated away from me into the darkness. I drank and took drugs. I took the boy and he took me. There was a hideous duality running through my body . . . I felt completely defeated and lost all notion of time and space. So where was I? I was hungry and thirsty for love. I was just a tiny point on the human horizon diminishing.[4]

The Prolongation of Adolescence

The plight of this young woman is made more pronounced because the duration of her adolescent confusion is constantly becoming more prolonged. Those points demarking the passage from childhood to adolescence—the onset of menstruation, the development of secondary sex characteristics, the use of brassieres, jocks, cosmetics, and dad's razor, the admission to the church, the age of legal majority—all of these, as well as dating and sexual involvements—have tended to move earlier and earlier into one's life. It is almost

98

as if our culture were in a hurry to make adults out of children, or at least to make adolescents out of them. Perhaps the most startling statistic involves the age of menarche, which would seem to be immune from societal pressures. There has been a continual drop in the age of menarche of about four months per decade since 1850. In 1850 the average age of first menstruation was fifteen; in 1950 it was twelve.[5]

But if the age of entering adolescence is being lowered, the age of leaving it is being raised. Those events which traditionally have marked a readiness to accept the full rights and responsibility of adulthood are being delayed. Marriage, conclusion of formal education, acceptance of full-time employment, the final and decisive break with the home—all these events are happening later and later.

Childhood is being left earlier and adulthood is being entered later. And in between is a stretch of six to sixteen years of adolescent liminality. Literally hoards of young people are over the threshold—*en passage*—but have not yet arrived. They are in the midst of a growth process that has no punctuation points. It feels like a run-on sentence. They can perceive no logic or purpose or progress—just relentless movement that gives them no time for rest and recuperation and leaves them exhausted.

The Dynamics of Adolescence

The exhaustion derives from trying to cope with the psychological dynamics at this stage in life. Adolescence is described by Anna Freud in its most rudimentary terms. It is like a second edition of early childhood; "both periods have in common the fact that a relatively strong id confronts a relatively weak ego."[7] Eric Erickson urges us to think of adolescence as

a normative crisis, i.e., a normal phase of increased conflict characterized by seeming fluctuation in ego strength and yet by high growth potential. What may appear to be the onset of a neurosis often is but an aggravated crisis which might prove to be self-liquidating and in fact contributive to the process of identity formation.[7]

Dr. Irene Josselyn, a noted psychiatrist and author, introduces us to the possibility that the task may be too demanding, at least at times.

The typical adolescent with some perceptiveness abandons his childhood identity and struggles to structure a new one, within the framework of his abilities and limitations, that will be compatible with his conception of adulthood . . . these tasks require a great deal of psychic energy and then the adolescent ego is at times exhausted.[8]

A commentator of the youth scene of 100 years ago—before the term adolescent had come into common usage—said it more simply. Separation from home "is a moral crisis that many of our youth do not show themselves able to meet. It comes at a tender age, when judgment is weakest and passion and impulse strongest."[9]

Ambivalence and Vacillation

In the early teenage years, there are strong internal urges and unprecedented external opportunities to experience more life, more excitement. The problem is in knowing how much the system can bear. If the young person takes on too much, he or she can be overwhelmed and will need to beat a hasty retreat back to some secure place—if the bridges to safety have not already been burned. If the person takes on too little, then the basic human needs for excitement will be unmet and may demand expression at some other, less opportune time.

But how can young people know what is too much and what is too little? The only way is to risk the journey through the turbulence, constantly making mid-course corrections.

Anyone who has lived with adolescents is aware of the endless swings back and forth in mood, in commitment, in enthusiasm. They live an exhausting ambivalence, and those who have a poorly developed sense of self—who seem to lack a solid center to their personality—swing from one extreme to another in endless alternation.

I recall many occasions when young people have exhausted *me* by taking me from one pole to another in trying to understand their relationship to me. Once, as I arrived at the church for a weekend retreat, I was greeted by a teenager racing up to me to ask my approval for his outfit and my permission to sit in the front seat of the car. Both requests struck me as rather childish. Even the tone of his voice caused me to wonder if he was in the midst of some regression. Within a few short hours, the boy—now acting very much like a man—sought me out for some private conversation. He was anxious about his thirteen year old girl friend. I remember his words. "She's not pregnant. That's not the issue. But she doesn't have much respect for herself. She uses her body in dumb ways. I'm afraid she's going to get hurt." In the same conversation, he demonstrated remarkable self-understanding.

> I feel confused. Sometimes I feel like a nine-year old. That's how they treat me at home. But when I'm with my real father, I feel really grown up. I like feeling grown up, but it doesn't seem real. I can't wait for this feeling to pass.

As I introduced him to the concept of ambivalence, assured him that the feeling would pass, and advised him not to rush the process, I felt as though he was well on the road to adulthood.

Thus, I was not prepared for the news that he had wandered away from the group for a cigarette, thereby violating our primary rule—stay together. When I discovered him, he quickly fabricated some story about his needing to check to see if anyone else had gone. Astounded by his tale, I asked him why he had lied to me. With an incredible burst of openness he answered, "Bill, I lied because I didn't want you to know the truth. I need your respect." Shortly after we returned home, this initiate called to tell me that his mother had been suddenly institutionalized. "But don't worry about my sister or me. I can take care of things at home."

Within a matter of two days this boy-man had psychologically covered a lot of ground. He moved from dependence to independence. He acted almost like a rebellious toddler within hours of a time when he would sound like a wise old man. I was exhausted just trying to keep up with him. Just imagine how *his* ego must have felt, continually adjusting and trying to control that inner turmoil. It must have been exhausted.

The ambivalence of adolescence pertains to almost every issue, even the central issue of the age—growing up. I became aware of these mixed feelings at a meeting when the initiates were unwilling to get serious, even though the evening's subject matter demanded optimal maturity. In exasperation I asked what I thought were rhetorical questions: "What's wrong with you tonight? Can't you stop giggling? Don't you ever want to grow up?"

In the silence that followed my outburst, I heard a sheepish, "No."

"What?" I asked.

"No; in a lot of different ways, I don't want to grow up."

We immediately abandoned the agenda announced for that session and turned our attention to the agenda set by this girl's honesty. We talked about the pressures of growing up.

- Pressures from peers: "I don't want to drink but when I go to parties they call me a little kid if I don't."
- Pressure from parents: "My mother and father keep telling me I'm getting just like my sister. She got in trouble, so everyone thinks when I grow up, I'll get in trouble. They're forcing me into a mold. And I don't want to fit it."
- Pressure from within: "I don't think I want to drive. I mean, I do and I don't. But it's scary to have that

responsibility of a steering wheel in your hand. There's something real nice about sitting in the back seat and being free."

The fact of the matter is that adolescence is a time of ambivalence, and everyone who is caught up in it will feel the endless movement in opposite directions:

- To be a unique individual as well as a fully-accepted member of the clan with severely circumscribed and distinctive norms for clothing, hair style, social life, and language.
- To be ready to try anything new, yet caught in repetitive behavior patterns and worn-out relationships.
- To live with intensity and still "be cool," feigning disinterest.
- To rebel and still hope, deep within you, that there will be something to go back to after the rebellion has passed.

As Eric Erikson said in an article on adolescent commitment:

> Diversity . . . and fidelity are polarized: they make each other significant and keep each other alive . . . Fidelity without a sense of diversity can become an obsession and a bore; diversity without a sense of fidelity, an empty relativism.[10]

Terrible Twos and Terrible Teens

In many ways, the years of adolescence are similar to the second year of life: the reign of the "terrible two-year-old," the time when toddlers become aware of themselves as separate from the world around them, when the impulses of a hyperactive id threaten to overwhelm the understaffed ego. Some of the same psychological devices are employed by the toddler and teenager—the most effective one being a well-developed negativism. To say "no" in word and deed is to set yourself apart and over against parents and other authorities who would try to mold you to fit into their image of you. And yet, if there were no image for you to reject, if

103

they simply did not recognize you or envision any hopes for you, then you would suffer much more acutely. One of the most insightful movies about adolescence dramatizes the dilemma. In *Rebel Without a Cause,* Jimmy—played by James Dean, a classic adolescent in his own life—pleads again and again with his father to tell him what to do. He wants to know the rules, the limits, the expectations. But his parents cannot give him what he wants. They shrink before his questions. His mother's only solution is to move the family to a different city every time Jimmy gets into trouble, hoping that a "new atmosphere" will cause Jimmy "to behave." His father's continual response is to try, once again, to understand. Their rebellious son is left to work out his problems for himself, in spite of his plea, "Please, Dad, just tell me what to do."

Anyone can sympathize with the parents. They are damned if they do and damned if they don't, wrong if they risk an answer and wrong if they don't. Yet most parents of teenagers survived the "terrible twos" and then marveled at the sense of self-certainty that had mysteriously come upon their child. Likewise, most parents will survive the plague of adolescence in spite of the oft-articulated desire to be spared its vicissitudes. "You ought to bury them at twelve and dig them up at eighteen," said one discouraged mother, momentarily ignoring the fact that the six years of conflict were a part of a growth process that must be survived and endured, and even at times relished and celebrated.

Adolescence as a Process

What this mother forgot is the central fact that we must never forget. Adolescence is a *process*. One cannot jump from childhood to adulthood in one nice, easy movement. One must pass through the turbulence. Only if one remains true to the task of one's age will one eventually pass out of it. The continual swings from one extreme to another do not contradict each other. Rather, they are embraced by the life of the adolescent, and enable him or her to grow more profoundly into adulthood.

It is like a ratchet screwdriver. You turn it as far as you can in one direction—the clockwise direction. Then you reverse your motion, seemingly negating all the effort you made to drive the screw into the wood. When you have gone in reverse as far as you can, then you again turn the screw in the clockwise direction. You repeat the process, over and again. As you do, the screw sinks ever more deeply until, finally, you have completed the task, and you can stop your effort or redirect it to a new challenge.

Adolescents go in one direction, then reverse themselves in what seems like perpetual contradiction. But as they move back and forth, they are testing limits, absorbing life, and growing more fully into their potential. Some day they will realize that the task of adolescence has been completed. We hope they will realize that it was worth it.

CHAPTER SIX

A Congregation Moves into the Wilderness

When Jesus went into the wilderness, he discovered that he not only was surrounded by wild beasts, but also was ministered unto by angels. Adolescence is a wilderness. It is filled with wild beasts. The church needs to enter the wilderness on the side of the angels, bringing a message of Christian concern. A congregation in Middletown had done that in a unique way.

The First Church of Christ

First Church is called First Church because it was the first church in Middletown. For the first one-hundred years it probably was called simply "the church," for it was the only church for miles around. Through its long history, this church has been one of the pillars of the city's social structure, even though the city has changed dramatically over the years. In the beginning, Middletown was a Congregational town. The first vote of the citizenry was to build a church, and for years all the activities of the town were voted in the church's ecclesiastical council. As time went on, that was to change. By the middle of the eighteenth century there were two other churches in town: The Church of England and the Strict

Congregational Church. These were at either end of the community, with olde First Church right in the center. By the middle of the nineteenth century, there were many churches, reflecting the growing ethnic variety of the city—Baptists, Methodists, German and Swedish Lutherans, Irish Catholics, and Black African Methodist Episcopalians—but First Church was still very much in the center of affairs. By the middle of the twentieth century, the ethnic influence became dominant. Middletown had become a haven for immigrants. In addition to the Germans, Swedes, Irish, and Blacks, there was an influx of Polish, Italians, and Hispanics—even Indians and Southeast Asians. In a city where there was once one church and everyone who worshiped went there, we now had more than thirty churches, and most people worshiped in one of the five Roman Catholic Churches. Olde First Church was no longer at the center of the city's life.

Adjustments to changes of this magnitude are never easy for a church. But First Church managed with reasonable grace and considerable good fortune. Our building is still lovely, functional, and in good repair. Our congregation has maintained a reasonable size—600 members with an average of 220 persons at worship each Sunday. The most significant event in the last twenty-five years was the decision to affiliate with the United Church of Christ. First Church has been able to retain its Congregational ways even as it has become aware of the need to welcome new ideas and new persons into our midst.

Another significant event in the recent past resulted from the rediscovery of the interrelatedness between Christian worship and Christian education. At First Church we believe that all persons of all ages need *both* worship and education. We have structured our life to reflect this belief.

For children, we have a number of programs: a pre-school program, the traditional church school with many untraditional flourishes, and children's worship. For young people we have the three youth programs—PIGs, Initiation Group, and Graduates—and church school. We expect the young people to worship with the adult congregation. For adults we have a high-powered education program during our second hour, frequent retreats and study groups, and regular worship. All this is held together with good music, a spirit of fellowship, and a concern for our fellow human beings.

Two components of our congregational life have particular relevance for understanding our initiation program: worship for children and education for adults.

Worship for Children

When our congregation gathers for worship at 10:00 a.m. on Sunday morning, everyone from the youngest to the oldest is together. Now that's not *quite* true. The very youngest are often in cribs, and the very oldest are often homebound and can only participate in the worship service via a telephone hookup. But most others are there in our big, old sanctuary.

After about fifteen minutes the children from kindergarten through fifth or sixth grade are invited to a special celebration of the word, which has been designed to allow them to express their faith in ways appropriate to their age. They use their imaginations. They use stories. They also use the liturgies of the faith and learn the basic patterns of all worship—they are separated from the mundane world and its concerns. They enter a sacred time and space to hear stories of the faith that relate to the concerns of the mundane world, and they return to that world informed and encouraged by their encounter with the faith.

During the course of each year in children's worship the children enter five different spaces and live out five different stages in the story of our faith.

● In the fall they become the Children of Israel, gathering around the campfire at the patriarch's tent, repeating the ancient confessions of faith as a password—"Who is your father?" "My father is a wandering Aramean"—learning the *Sh'ma Israel*—"Hear O Israel, the Lord your God is One . . ."

—memorizing the 23rd Psalm, singing folk tunes, and, most importantly, meeting the heroes and heroines of the faith: Abraham and Sarah, Isaac and Rebecca, Jacob and Rachel, Joseph and his brothers, Moses, Sampson and Deborah and Samuel, Saul and David, Elijah and Ezekiel. Week after week, these giants from the past are presented to awaken the heroic in the child.

● In Advent the children are transported to Babylon where they become the people of the exile, gathered around the Advent wreath at "Isaiah's hovel" in the slaves' ghetto. With the help of password and biblical verses, prayers and carols, they meet the hopes of the season as we move closer and closer to the coming of the Prince of Peace.

● During Epiphany the children become the early church. This time they meet in a private home in Rome, say their password in Latin—*Pax vobiscum,*—and learn the stories of the life of Jesus through weekly visits of Andrew and James, Martha and Mary, Mary Magdelene and even Mary, the Mother of Jesus. The children get so caught up in the experience that sometimes intrusions from the outside must be dismissed summarily. On one occasion when Mary was asked a question about Jesus' boyhood and the minister tried to rescue the visiting thespian from her distress, a child quickly reminded the pastor of his place: "Would you please let her answer! She knows more than you! She's his mother, you know!"

● If children are caught up in the flow of things in Epiphany, they are even more so in Lent. Beginning with the Sunday before Ash Wednesday, we hear talk about persecution. Shortly thereafter it becomes necessary to be secretive about our faith. We move to the catacombs. For passwords we use the sign of the fish and resurrection liturgies:

"He is risen," says one.

"He is risen indeed," answers the other.

And Sunday after Sunday we are emboldened by the stories of the Passion of our Lord.

• In the weeks following Easter, we move into the later history of the church, living out other moments in the passage of our faith. Some years we become monks. Other years, reformers. Sometimes we are those first settlers in Middletown, worshiping in a log meeting house. Some years we move through our different traditions, becoming Baptists, on the occasion of a baptism, Episcopalians at morning prayer, Greek Orthodox at their Easter vigil. Still other years we move around the world, worshiping in Africa one week and Korea the next. There seems to be no end to what we can become in children's worship!

Education for Adults

It is also true that there is no end to what we can do in adult education, although it was somewhat difficult to get started. In 1970 a planning group proposed a change in the way the congregation gathered each Sunday. Rather than meeting for one hour—worship for adults and education for children— the proposal suggested we meet for two hours: worship for everyone in the first hour and education for everyone in the second. The reaction was mixed. A substantial number of people argued against it.

"We can't do that. We've always met for one hour. No one will come. Adults are finished with their church school, anyway. And the kids will be bored."

There was no way to counter those arguments head on, so a compromise resolution was passed. We tried it for one year.

The first year we worked hard to build the adult education program. We did two things that were wise. First, we offered several options, including the option to share a second cup of coffee and talk informally with one another. Second, we found excellent leaders who could teach us "the mysteries and techniques of adulthood," not just any "mystery and technique," but the ones about which we really wanted to learn.

In that first year, a highly political Roman Catholic priest taught us the Old Testament from the perspective of liberation theology, a psychologist led us to a higher level of sophistication in thinking about families, and the minister convened a group to discuss the morning sermon and service. By the end of the trial year, Adult Second Hour, as the program came to be called, was an integral part of our congregation's life. Through the years we have learned about all types of matters: liturgy, models of our faith, South Africa, the prophets, unemployment, divorce, death, medical ethics, the Boat People, and many more. It is evident to all who participate in Second Hour that the Lord always has "yet more light to break forth from his word," to quote our Congregational forebear, John Robinson. Or, to use the language of initiation, which the congregation often uses, we adults were given some exposure to the mysteries and techniques of adulthood as we grew up. The most we were given, however, was "entry level" knowledge. We must always expand our knowledge and refine our skills. We will always be *en passage.*

Programs for Adolescents

To support those who are passing through adolescence, First Church has developed three separate but integrally related programs. The keystone of our total effort is the Initiation Group. On one side is the Pre-Initiation Group, usually referred to as PIGs. On the other side are the Graduates, including all persons who have passed through their initiation.

The existence of these three groups serves as a continual reminder that growth is an ongoing process. Children in third and fourth grade can feel themselves getting older as they project forward to that sacred year when they will enter the Initiation Group. PIGs can see the rights and responsibilities accorded their immediate seniors and take solace from the knowledge that they, too, will eventually be given those rights and responsibilities. Initiates just live it out. The Graduates

111

can look back on where they have been and feel a genuine sense of accomplishment in the mere fact that they survived the first years of adolescence. Adults of all ages can recall their own passage to adulthood and see more closely the passages appropriate to their age in the so-called "predictable crises of adult life."

The Age of Initiation

The fact is that everyone in our congregation can derive some benefit from the initiation rite, but the primary beneficiaries are clearly the initiates themselves. We have chosen to offer the most intensive experience in the congregation's life to persons in eighth and ninth grades, who will be in ninth and tenth grade for the second year of the initiation. We have decided on this age group for several reasons:

1. *Tradition.* It was previously the tradition of the congregation to have a "Pastor's Class" in preparation for confirmation sometime during a student's freshman year in high school.

2. *Scheduling Conflicts.* We have found that the expectations of coaches, band directors, club advisors, teachers, and employers escalate during the last two years of high school; we feel it best to offer Initiation before those other commitments are undertaken.

3. *Needs of Adolescents.* The early years of adolescence are ones of dramatic physical growth and psychological confusion. They are marked by excessive privacy. These are the years when emerging adults desperately need stabilizing influences and a trusted community.

4. *Needs of the Parents.* Mothers and fathers—especially those whose oldest child is an emerging teenager—are often thrown by the sudden maturation and the deep ambivalence that is characteristic of the age. The Initiation Group gives these parents the assurance that their children

are in some structure that promotes responsible growth. The group, coincidentally, also gives parents a community of peers—the other parents—with which to share the passage. This parental peer group sometimes stays intact through the later teenage years.

The Ingredients of Initiation

When the time for the two-year initiation arrives, we take whatever ingredients we have and mix them together. We know that we need five things:
1. A special space.
2. A certain amount of time.
3. An adolescent peer group of any size.
4. A number of carefully selected adults.
5. A structure for an initiation.
Let us look at each of these components.

Space

A special space is important. In order to widen horizons, the group often will move out of its home base, but the group gains security by having a special place that can be called home. In our building, we found a previously unused room in the basement, next to a small gymnasium and the furnace room. It had cracked tiles on the floor, chipped paint on the walls, overstuffed furniture and an ancient phonograph. We converted it into a home for the Initiation Group. Each new group puts its own distinctive mark on the room, rearranging furniture, painting walls, decorating it according to their tastes. The room is marginal, but it has an aura of sacredness about it. Without anyone ever saying so, it has become "off limits" for adults—especially parents—and for children—especially PIGs.

Time

Reserved time is an essential ingredient. Our group's covenant is to meet twice a week, supplemented with

113

periodic, frequent retreats. Consistent attendance at the meetings and retreats is imperative. If one knows that one's peers will be present at the meetings, then one can risk trusting them to be present in other ways. If they are present in other ways, then there is a good chance they will support one in daring to speak the hopes and fears of this turbulent time of life. But if they will not give their time, then no one will take the chance of trusting and sharing. The initiation cannot work without time. Therefore, both young and old need to agree at the outset. "This is our time together. It is precious. It cannot be taken from us."

I have guided four initiation groups, each one very different from the others. In each group, attendance was good—well over 90 percent. But at varying points in each of the four experiences, there was a slippage. I could see that truancy was contagious and demoralizing. I knew the situation had degenerated too far in one group when a girl blurted out her true feelings. "I'm not going to share with them. I don't trust them. They haven't been here in two weeks." A month later, after I had summoned them back to the terms of their covenant, that deep caring came easily. The attendance had improved. The trust had returned. They were a group once again.

Adolescent Peers

Space and time are the first two ingredients. An adolescent peer group is the third. It is more important than most of us think. During the course of our initiation, adolescents learn to give themselves to one another. They listen. They respond. They care deeply for one another.

I saw this self-sharing again and again in our first Initiation Group. But it was most evident on the occasion when the only group couple broke up. The separation occurred on a Saturday night. The next morning, during the first hymn, I noticed the girl sitting alone, which struck me as unusual because she was normally with her beau. After the hymn, I

114

noticed that another member of the group was with her. For a moment I wondered if something was wrong, but thought little more about it. The organ postlude had not yet ended when I was told what happened. With tears in her eyes, she informed me that the romance had ended. I listened and tried to comfort her. Finally, I delivered her into the care of her friend and set about the rest of my pastoral duties, hoping that the members of the group would care for her and her hurting boy friend.

That night, in the regular group meeting, when other initiates talked about *their* feelings and behavior that day, I knew that my hopes had been met:

"When I saw her sitting alone in church, I knew something was wrong. Not because she was alone. It was just something about her. I couldn't stand it. I just had to do something. That's why I went and sat with her."

Another said, "I called him this afternoon. He said he just couldn't come tonight. He hurts too much. But he told me to tell you all that he'll be back soon."

As I watched these young people struggling with those awkward feelings—even daring to act on them—I thought of all those persons going through divorce who feel isolated from the sources of support and compassion that they need so badly. As we talked about divorce, some of the initiates began to empathize with their divorced parents in new and more meaningful ways.

In another Initiation Group, a girl began to have gnawing doubts about her attractiveness. The year prior to entering the initiation she had had a steady boy friend who subsequently had moved away. Now she had nothing except secret fears about herself. She nursed that secret as long as she felt necessary. Then in an astonishing act of trust, she decided to share her secret. She chose a fellow initiate—a boy whose judgment and sensitivity she had come to trust. She called him, told him her fears, and listened as he gently alleviated them.

Keeping and sharing secrets is an important part of growing up. Paul Tournier, the Swiss theologian doctor, writes about secrets:

Keeping a secret is the first step in the formation of the individual; telling it to a freely chosen confidant is going to constitute then the second step in this formation of the individual. Freedom is what makes the individual. Keeping a secret is an early assertion of freedom; telling it to someone that one chooses is going to be a later assertion of freedom, of even greater value. He who cannot keep a secret is not free. But he who can never reveal it is not free either . . . . This double action of withdrawal and giving of self is going to be repeated throughout a person's life and on every occasion. In order to give one's self, it is necessary to possess one's self; but it serves no useful purpose to possess one's self, if it is not in order to be able to give one's self.[1]

The process of keeping and sharing secrets continues throughout life. The caring and trusting that develops within the Initiation Group also should endure. I once received a call from a distraught mother whose son had been arrested and charged with several petty but potentially serious offenses. He had graduated out of the initiation program several years before, but as I sat with him in the police station, listening to his agony and alerting him to the folly of his ways, I was acutely aware of my personal limitation. I quickly realized how to expand my limits. I called another adult who had been part of the team that had guided the initiation, and I called his closest friend in the old peer group. The adult could give counsel. The age mate could give friendship. The juvenile offender, as he was about to be labeled, needed both.

In the formation of the peer group, it is important to be aware of conscious or unconscious labeling. Inevitably, some persons will emerge as leaders and others as followers, some as responsible persons and others as troublemakers. Stay attuned to ways in which counter-productive behavior is being reinforced. Mark Twain maintained that the town drunk was an elected official. What he meant was that forces conspire to trap people in roles, especially if we are insensitive to those forces. A healthy family is one with a rotating scapegoat, where psychological energy—positive or negative—does not focus exclusively on one child at the expense of the others. The same principle applies to an Initiation Group. If one person seems to be locked into unhealthy patterns that cause his or her self concept to suffer, you may need to change the course of the program to highlight or dramatize that person's strengths no matter how limited. Identity, good or bad, will be formed, at least in part, by the group's interaction. The group, therefore, must take seriously its potential to form identity. The abuse or misuse of this potential can have long-lasting effects.

Adult Leaders

The task of steering the initiation resides with the adult advisors. They, in a sense, assume the awesome role of the ancient novice masters, who traveled to the heights and the depths, who suffered but survived numerous initiation experiences in their own lives, and, who therefore, were chosen to show the path to adulthood.

In many ways, the modern task is more demanding than the ancient one. Our life is more complex. The confusion of adolescents is greater. The vision of adulthood is blurred. The landmarks along the trail are covered over. The pitfalls are camouflaged. There are few precedents of similar programs. Finally, few adults can look back to their own adolescence and see any coherent initiation.

In our initiation at First Church we experimented with different numbers and types of adult leaders. We have discovered that some configurations of personalities work better than others.

Our first effort was directed by an adult who was supported by another couple and by other adults who could be coopted for special assignments. This arrangement put too much pressure on the primary leader.

In our second attempt, therefore, we enlisted four persons to lead the group. Once again these four were to involve other adults as they saw fit. This, likewise, was less than satisfactory. We discovered that planning with four persons was cumbersome and time-consuming. Authority was diffused, and personal relationships were so diluted that they lost their effectiveness.

The problem of authority surfaced first. In working with teenagers one must constantly respond to their needs—either by comforting those who seem afflicted or by afflicting those who are comfortable, to paraphrase an age-old definition of the church's function. But when one is responding to an adolescent, or to a *group* of adolescents, one often cannot tell the difference between the afflicted and the comfortable. It becomes a matter of personal judgment whether one should correct the course by coddling and comforting, or by prodding and confronting. Yet the decisions must be made quickly, while the precipitating situation is fresh. One person is exhausted doing that. Four become confused.

The key to this dilemma was a question of dependency. When we worked with a quartet of leaders, we diluted the dependency at the very time we should have met those needs. Adolescents struggle to become independent of their parents. Consequently they need to transfer some of their strong feelings from their parents to other adults. In doing so they hope to get a more objective point of view on their lives. They can reveal their problems and seek advice without the deep emotional tie that creates guilt because of disagreement, or—paradoxically—because of compliance. Their search for another adult—a significant other—who can fulfill these dependency needs is often frustrated by our educational system at the very time when the needs become most pressing. All through the elementary school, the student has one teacher for a year and that teacher is able to develop a

118

reasonable knowledge of and a substantial personal relationship with the student. But in middle school or junior high school the pattern changes. There is no one parent-surrogate to know the student. Now there are many teachers each of whom specializes in knowing subjects, not students, and with whom it is more difficult to establish a deep relationship.

In our initiation, we consciously allow—indeed invite—a transference to develop between the adolescents and the adults. Following the wisdom of psychotherapy, we expect the initiates to project onto the initiators those feelings about adults—especially about parents—which are too unsettling to handle outside of this privileged relationship. We accept those feelings into our group and share the struggle to resolve them. We are conscious, however, that eventually the responsibility for those feelings and those relationships must be passed back to the adolescents. To help this to happen, we dilute the transference by designing our program to involve more and more adults as the end of the relationship nears. When a dependency is transferred from one person to several persons, it often matures into genuine independence.

The model of adult leadership that we found most effective was that of a team, with players having different roles and responsibilities as follows:

• There are two team leaders who are responsible for the entire initiation process. The two primary leaders—one male and one female—relate to the initiation and the initiates intensely over a two-year period.
• There is a cadre of adults who specialize in one or more of the four broad subject areas—Society, Sexuality, Spirituality, and the Self. These adults are involved in their special units and in all retreats and mystery rites.

The use of two primary leaders has given us more flexibility in responding to the ever-changing moods and needs of the initiates, singly or corporately. One leader can confront, while the other waits with the open heart of a comforter. The additional adults provide necessary relief to the primary leaders: retreats can be led by the others; whole units can be designed by the others; and, most important, the initiates come to know other models of Christian adulthood.

Whatever configuration is used, all adults must be selected with great care. The single most important factor in the formation of a person's faith is the faith of the catechist who is with that person in the moment of receptivity. In addition, there are some qualities to be sought and others to be avoided in the adult leaders.

● Beware, for instance, of "the older brother" personality type, so ingeniously depicted in the parable of the prodigal son. In this parable, the older brother, who had never swerved from the narrow path, rejected his brother in his wandering away and in his return home. The older brother assumed self-righteously that his younger brother should be like him.

Our churches have a fair number of "older brothers," adults with overstrict consciences who failed to resolve the challenges of adolescence. Very often, because of a fascination with that stage of life which still is unfulfilled, these persons volunteer to lead youth groups. If they are chosen, they vacillate between encouraging rebellion by their almost voyeuristic interest and stifling it by pronouncements from their rigid code. Either way, they distort the process.

● Beware of persons whose intimacy needs are not being met. Teenagers have a great sexual appeal. Furthermore, they often develop toward the adult leaders strong feelings which are sexually tinged. They allow these feelings to develop in part because the leaders are viewed as safe—that is, the leaders are in control of the situation and would not allow the feelings inappropriate expression. If, however, the leaders cannot control their own feelings, a dangerous set of circumstances prevails. There is a chance that irreparable damage will be done to the persons and to the program.

● Finally, beware of any adult who believes that somehow he

or she will achieve fame and glory from leading the Initiation Group. The reverse is more likely to be true. He or she will know abuse and failure—or at least frustration. One of the most necessary qualities for leaders is the capacity to withstand conflict, to possess the security of having accomplished their own passage to adulthood so that they can risk having it challenged and even rejected. Sigmund Freud observed this in terms of therapy, "No one who dares to tame the wild beasts that inhabit the human beast can expect to remain unscathed."[2] Erik Erickson made us conscious of this same dynamic between generations:

> No longer is it merely for the old to teach the young the meaning of life, whether individual or collective. It is the young, who, by their responses and actions, tell the old whether life as represented by the old and as presented to the young has meaning; and it is the young who carry in them the power to confirm those who confirm them, and joining the issues, to renew and to regenerate, or to reform and to rebel.[3]

In order to initiate, the leaders should expect to be initiated; in order to foster adolescents to wholeness of adulthood, they should expect to be broken; in order to invest young people with a functional value system, they must expect their own values to be questioned and rejected.

As if the rejections from the initiates were not enough, the adult leaders should expect some hostility—or at least ambivalence—from the parents of the initiates. In the initiation program, parents are allowing another to get close to their children at the very time when they are often frustrated and threatened by the growing distance from their children. Mothers, who classically have given so much of their life to nurturing children, feel that which has given them purpose and meaning to be slipping away from them. Fathers who may be redirecting energy from their jobs to their families, often find that their children want to be free from the family and are embarrassed by the father's efforts to be tender. Just when the parents are opening up, the children are closing them out, projecting onto the parents much of their internal chaos as they discard the ways of childhood and move to become a man or a woman.

But even with this foreknowledge of possible rejection, by initiates and parents, the adult leaders must still have the faith to become vulnerable, to tell their story, and to express their values. In this way, they provide the raw material—the human information—that can be assimilated by the teenagers as they form their own values and create their own lives. Adult leaders need to share the scars of their own adolescence and the wounds of the adult life. As they do, they illumine the path that the initiates must travel.

I remember an occasion when a boy had suffered a somewhat severe setback and rejection from some friends at school. He came to the meeting, but he did not enter in completely. He seemed to be licking his wounds off in the corner. Someone asked him what was wrong. He said that we could never understand, we had never known rejection. Hoping that he might benefit from hearing one of the most painful memories of my high school days, I told the following story:

> I had been elected class president and earned a starting position on our wrestling squad. And I had to pay for my victories. The defeated candidate for president teamed up with my primary wrestling opponent and phoned me to threaten me with physical violence. None came. But the next morning I suffered devastating psychological violence when I saw myself hanging in effigy in front of the school door.

When I told the tale—with no more detail than is reported here—my rejected initiate discovered the points of shared suffering. That freed him to open up and to let the group help him. Many adolescents don't see adults suffer. They're intimidated by adult competence. They need to be told that their loneliness, awkwardness, and fear of failure are known by people of all ages. They are the common lot of humanity.

It should be obvious even from this incomplete survey of some of the traits necessary for effective leadership, that any chosen for the task must have an abiding faith. They will enter a world which is filled with chaos. Yet they have to believe that God's creative spirit is at work amidst all the confusion. They will open themselves to rejection and hurt. So they have to believe that "the garment of Christ," which they put on in baptism, will somehow enable them to bear their vulnerability. They will find their values, their faith, their lives questioned. So they will need to be reasonably sure that their own adulthood has integrity and is consonant with the standard that we proclaim to the world—including adolescents—that of Jesus Christ.

Many particulars of the faith can be gleaned from books and outside resources, but living testimony can be given only by those who covenant to share their lives with the initiates.

CHAPTER SEVEN

A Way Through The Wilderness— A Contemporary Initiation to Christian Adulthood

At First Church in Middletown we have developed a structure to assist us in initiating young people to Christian adulthood. It is not a rigid structure. It cannot be. The realities of the world in which we live keep changing. The persons who pass through the initiation are unique. The corporate personality of each Initiation Group is distinct. Even the adult leaders vary from one experience to the next. And the congregation is in constant flux, with changing resources and limitations. So our structure is necessarily flexible. Some general comments can be made, however. There are discernible movements that can be described, and there is a wealth of experiences that can be shared.

Our initiation includes between twelve and twenty-five young people who commit themselves to meet twice a week for two years; they also go on frequent retreats.

Our initiation also has a cadre of about six adults and the

resources of the entire congregation. It does not cost much money. But it does take time.

Our initiation derives its most basic purpose and pattern from primitive puberty rites: It seeks to impart minimal knowledge about the mysteries and techniques of adulthood, and it employs the classic rhythm of all rites of passage—separation, transition, and reincorporation. That motif, like the theme of a fugue, recurs again and again. It is played out over the biennium. The entire process begins with a rite of separation, and it ends, after a lengthy journey, with a rite of incorporation. Each of the four units also is shaped by the separation-transition-incorporation pattern. Likewise, many of the individual sessions and all of the retreats and mystery rites follow this same progression.

The two-year initiation rite includes within it a wide range of activities: lectures, group discussions, Bible study, Bible sculpture, campfire discussions, private conversations, tests, quizzes, research, homework, prayer, singing, motion pictures, interviews, retreats, and mystery rites.

The mystery rites are the most unusual. There are eight of them. They have been developed in an attempt to use ritual as a means to move learning into the more mysterious realms of human experience. The eight rites are: the Rite of Separation, the Urban Adventure, the Encounter with Silence, the Masking Ritual, the Sexuality Rite, the Ash Wednesday Service, the Wilderness Experience, and the Final Act of Initiation.

Candidates for initiation are given information about the experience in a three-week introduction. During that time we

- Learn about initiations through a preliminary lecture on primitive customs and a visit from Jewish age peers who are Bar Mitzvah.
- Meet one another by playing a number of group-forming games.
- Talk with parents. At the parents' meeting we answer

questions, solicit support, and beg tolerance of a certain amount of secrecy.

The adult leaders always have asked the parents to trust us. During the next two years, their children will share many secrets with us. We want to be able to protect those confidences. On the other hand, we do not wish to bind ourselves totally to a vow of secrecy, for such a vow might compromise our effectiveness in stopping destructive—especially self-destructive—behavior. We learned this from experience. Initially I thought it was important to set down absolutes regarding confidences: Under no circumstances would I share personal material from the group; the parents were prohibited from inquiring.

As time went on, several isolated instances led me to amend that position. The first was one in which parents were feeling threatened by their son's unpredictable moods. They asked me to meet with the whole family. I asked the boy's permission before sitting down with the family. Another time, I received a visit from a worried father, whose anxieties and suspicions about his daughter were misplaced. I used my own judgment in consenting to talk with him, but I never mentioned the conversation to the girl.

These may seem like minor matters, but the triangle between parent-child/initiate-initiator is one that needs to be recognized and dealt with in a conscious way. If the trust is fairly strong around the triangle, the conditions are ripe for a successful initiation. If the trust is weak, the purposes of initiation may be thwarted.

After the parents' meeting, the initiates go off on their first retreat, during which we eat, sing, worship, play, and talk further about the experience that lies ahead. Some of us even sleep, although it has become an unwritten rule that adolescents spend the night talking around the campfire. During this retreat the Initiation Group is being formed. We are preparing for the first mystery rite.

126

The Rite of Separation

The rite of separation is an adaptation of three initiation rites, two ancient and one modern.

● The Masai people of Kenya begin their initiation by taking boys of several villages to the camp of the medicine man, who divides them into two age groups. The younger boys are allowed to watch as the older ones are taken out of the ranks of the children and led away to become warriors.

● The Pueblo Indians of the American Southwest believe that the journey will take them through the land of the dead. In order to relate to their departed ancestors, the novices must paint themselves white to personify ghosts.

● An honorary society at an Eastern university takes its neophytes out to a sacred glen bisected by a stream that separates the men from the boys. The stream can be crossed only if a riddle is solved. After the passage is successfully negotiated, a meal is shared as the old and the new become one community.

For our rite of separation, an invitation is extended to the entire congregation, with four groups given special invitations—the Pre-Initiation Group (PIGs), the Candidates for Initiation, the Graduates, and the parents of all three groups.

When the congregation arrives, they are met by the novice masters, who first call the Graduates and send them over the threshold to a place where selected adults await the arrival of the initiates.

Then the drama begins. One at a time the PIGs are escorted by the parents to the guru, who confronts them with the question: "Have you been to Penuel?"

"What?" answers the first child. "That is not the correct answer," replies the leader, and with feigned disappointment and condescension, he advises the young PIG to go back to his parents for two years and then come and try again. As the rejected child leaves he hears the taunt: "Now hold on to your daddy's hand. You're still a child. But come again in two years."

After the PIGs have been rejected appropriately, the initiates are brought forth by their parents. Once again the question is asked, "Have you been to Penuel?"

Once again the response is inevitably, "What?" But now everything is changed.

"I notice an inquisitive nature," observes the leader. "Are you ready to pass on to adulthood?"

"Yes, sir."

"Father, Mother, take your child over the threshold. Bid him goodbye. He is a child no longer. In two years you can have him back. But he will be different. And you will be, too. Join the other parents in weeping for the death of your child."

With those instructions, the parents follow the course that parents have followed for years. As the younger children watch wide-eyed, the parents deliver their child to the fate that awaits, say goodbye with a kiss, hug, or handshake, and gather with the other parents who helplessly see their offspring humbled, blindfolded, dusted with powder to make them white like the dead, then packed in a van and taken away.

Where they go no one knows. Every town and city has its own streams and glens waiting to be made sacred by the arrival of a new generation of initiates. Our mystical forest has played its role for years and it plays it very well. Its primary features are its darkness and its almost primeval nature. It has a small brook that bubbles through it, creating over the centuries a steep slope on one side and an outcropping of rock on the other. When the initiates arrive, they are still blindfolded and very quiet. They have no idea where they are. They have no idea what they are to do. They have no idea who they are. They are truly liminal beings. They have crossed the threshold of a new existence and they are lost.

Into the silent darkness comes a voice. "Hear, O people. You who are blind, open your eyes that they may see."

Then another voice. "Hear, O people. You who are dead, have courage that you may live."

And finally, "Hear O people. You who are deaf and dumb, listen and speak to one another that you may learn."

Then, one at a time they are brought down the slope, asked questions about the riddle they, as individuals and as a group must solve, and sent back up the hill to share with their brothers and sisters what they have learned. Eventually they may even know enough to cross over the stream.

Our ritual uses as the material for its riddle the story of Jacob at Penuel, as found in Genesis 32. That story is chosen because it is a classic rite of passage involving a change of ontological status, signified by a change of name (Jacob becomes Israel), a struggle, a self limiting (Jacob is lamed), a river crossing, a blessing. There are many other stories that can be used equally effectively. Noah's Ark, the Binding of Isaac, the Exodus, the 40 Years in the Wilderness of the People of Israel, the Baptism of Jesus, the Transfiguration. In each case, the questions would be asked of the neophytes, and the answers must also be given to them. They, after all, are barely out of childhood and a long way from being able to deal maturely with such adult themes. They will have to be nurtured. If necessary—or perhaps by design—one of the more comforting adults may sneak to the other side of the stream and help the initiates along. One way or the other they will be helped to answer the riddle.

And then, they are helped across the stream, received into a community of adults, washed of their clay and dust, and offered a meal.

The first act of initiation is over. They were separated from their parents, taken to an unknown and frightening place, made to feel incompetent, given enough information to solve a riddle, led through the waters, and welcomed to their new status by sharing the warmth of the fire and the fellowship of a meal.

At deeper levels of the psyche, the most archetypal dynamics of human growth were being activated. The neophytes were all killed off and born again. They were crossing the waters that separated the old from the new, the children from the adults. Once they were on the other side, they were committed to the new. They had been taken back to the beginning and led by the hand to a point where they could almost see with their own eyes, almost stand on their own two feet, and almost understand with their own being.

They do not understand fully. No one does. The experience through which they pass on the occasion of their separation from childhood is a mystery rite, the first of eight. The mystery rites allow them to probe the unknown; to feel its impact on their lives; to experience the progression from being blind to seeing, from being foolish to being successful, from being isolated to being accepted, from being too young to risk the initiation to being mature enough. But even though the mystery rites reveal much about life's mysteries, they conceal just as much. The initiates walk away, shaking their heads in a combination of awe and disbelief-belief. They are now ready for their journey to adulthood.

The Journey into Understanding

The journey which the initiates pursue takes them through four broad areas: (1) the society in which they live, (2) the self as a unique, historical being, (3) sexuality, and (4) spirituality.

The Unit on Society

The journey into understanding begins with the unit on society for several reasons. First, the group's trust level is low. There is less personal risk in sharing political views and debating the strengths of political candidates and platforms than in revealing secrets and confusion about one's self, sexuality, or spirituality. At this stage, in spite of all the enthusiasm and excitement, there is little trust. We need more time together to achieve trust.

Second, the relation between church and society deserves priority consideration. This is easy to forget, especially when working with adolescents, whose precipitous self and sexual development is fascinating to both adolescents and their mentors. But, as one churchman argued, "The church needs to train its people to *think* politically, socially, economically, theologically, and ethically."[1] That need is so great it should be considered first and foremost.

Third, the unit on society begins with politics. The best time to learn the techniques and mysteries of our political system is in the weeks leading up to an election. So that is when we do it.

Before we begin, the novice masters try to identify their own biases. In this entire initiation program we try to present values and value judgments as clearly as possible. Public school teachers are, supposedly, prohibited from impos-ing—or even presenting—personal values. They are contin-ually admonished to be objective, to let the students decide.

Not only is such value-free education impossible, it is basically unwise. It is better to be open about one's prejudices, to take a position, to explain why it was chosen, and then to defend it—not with arrogant defensiveness but with self-affirmed openness. I have found in eight years of intense interaction with the initiates, preceded by several years of general youth work, that adolescents appreciate the person who stands for something unashamedly.

My own bias, when it comes to politics, economics, and social justice, favors the disenfranchised, the poor, the oppressed. I believe that is the bias appropriate to the Christian. It is the commission that Jesus of Nazareth accepted when he began his public ministry.

> So he came to Nazareth, . . . and went to synagogue on the
> Sabbath day as he regularly did. He stood up to read the lesson

and was handed the scroll of the prophet Isaiah. He opened the scroll and found the passage which says, "The spirit of the Lord is upon me because he has anointed me; he has sent me to announce good news to the poor, to proclaim release for prisoners and recovery of sight for the blind; to let the broken victims go free, to proclaim the year of the Lord's favour" (Luke 4:16–20 NEB).

Once this bias is clearly stated, the unit on society can begin.

The unit has several sub-units. In any given initiation, we will deal with three or four of the following topics: politics, economics, urbanization, inter-cultural relations, racism, disarmament, our legal system, peace, prisons, care of the physically and mentally handicapped. For each of these sub-units, we have created learning packages that include the following:

- A list of terms with which the initiates must converse wisely.
- A set of issues about which the initiates must become knowledgeable.
- Some learning games.
- Some resources.
- Some opportunities to become acquainted with practitioners in the field.

For the sub-unit on politics, for instance, we send a memo that describes the terms and issues that the initiates need to know. Included is the schedule by which we guide the group to the necessary knowledge. A portion of the memo prepared prior to the 1980 election reads as follows:

During the next month you will be expected to become knowledgeable about the upcoming election. In addition to reading the newspaper and news magazines regularly, you should attend all group meetings during which we will discuss different biblical passages that deal with the role of politics, meet with Republican and Democratic candidates for local office, select a presidential candidate, work under the direction of active politicians in campaign headquarters, watch a televised debate of the presidential nominees, prepare ourselves to debate the merits of our candidate and his platform, stage our own debate, observe the closing of a polling place on election eve, and join in a party to watch the early returns on television and celebrate your candidate's victory or commiserate in his defeat.

For *our* debate you should be conversant about the major issues of the campaign. The best way to prepare is to know the meaning of the following terms, and when applicable, to know your candidate's position in regard to them:

SALT II	Moral Majority
Strategic Arms	Gun Control
Conventional Weapons	Abortion
Disarmament	Supreme Court
Straits of Hormuz	Doxology
Hostages	Platform
P.L.O.	Income Tax
Spirit of Camp David	Balanced Budget
Panama Canal Treaty	Charisma
Unemployment	Leadership
Inflation	Supply Side Economics
E.R.A.	Civil Rights

You should also be prepared to explain the relationship between your candidate's platform and what has been called "The Christian's Platform." (Look it up for yourself—Luke 4:16–20). Does your candidate have "good news" for the poor? Whom does your candidate consider to be oppressed? Whom does he identify as the victims of our social order? How would he help them?

The memo outlined the course that we would follow to a destination that we had identified. By the time of the election the initiates were to know what was happening. On the Sunday before the election, we used the initiates' debate as a means of testing the group—and having some good fun at the same time. The initiates are seated at tables—Republicans on one side, Democrats on the other, Independents in the middle. In front of them sit several adults invited to serve as journalists inquiring about foreign and domestic policy as well as the candidates' personal beliefs. Another adult serves as host—welcoming the television audience, monitoring the time, and asking for clarification of points. As the debate rages, the initiates struggle to use the language of adulthood. They always seem to surprise themselves with their capacity for maturity.

When the host calls an end to the debate and thanks the participants for their cooperation, the focus of attention turns to the adult interviewers who are instantaneously transformed into expert commentators. In the next few minutes, as the young people listen with rapt attention, the adults converse with one another. They give their own opinions about the responses of the candidates, pointing out where they were unclear on the issues, elaborating on some of the points, and finally, applauding the efforts of those who have learned so much so quickly.

The evening ends on that note. It's been fun. It's been hard work. It's been a good learning experience. The initiates know much more about the techniques and mysteries of our political system. They have taken significant steps to becoming responsible citizens.

The significance of those steps can be overlooked easily. Even I might have overlooked it if the initiates themselves had not reminded me time and again. The most vivid reminder was given by one young woman in the group who happened to be born with Down's Syndrome.

I should point out that in all four Groups we had a wide range of intellectual and personal gifts, from award winning scholars and athletes to persons with severe learning and physical limitations. Those who were most limited in traditional academic terms were frequently the best learners and teachers of life's toughest lessons. They knew about tragedy. They had far more wisdom than their more fortunate brothers and sisters.

That was certainly evident on the night when we were taught one of the fundamental facts of life about adult responsibility. It was a night I have already mentioned when speaking of the ambivalence associated with growing up. There was something comfortable about staying a child: less pressure, less responsibility, much easier.

As that talk continued, our Down's Syndrome initiate, who had struggled so hard to grow up, was becoming increasingly agitated. Finally she stood up and, pounding her chest, blurted out something that sounded like "I dul!"

"What?" I asked.

"I dul! I adult!"

"Say it slowly so we can understand."

"I adult, Bill. Look at me. I big. I am adult. When I watch TV news, I understand. Little Robbie, he doesn't understand the news. I understand! I am an adult!"

In a moment like that, there is nothing to do but blink back the tears of joy and amazement and pray that the lesson she had so eloquently taught was learned by the others. You cannot be a responsible citizen without first understanding what is happening. Learn the language. Know the techniques. Get in touch with the mysterious ways by which our society functions.

Politics is just one of the ways to understand the mysteries of our society. So we have created and continue to create sub-units on other topics. Most of these sub-units contain the type of challenge found in the one on politics. One component not found in the sub-unit on politics is found in many of the others. We have discovered a handful of simulation games that help deepen the awareness of the initiates to moral issues. Four of the best are:

- *Plea Bargaining,* which provides a vivid introduction to our legal system.
- *Baldicer,* which deals with world hunger.
- *Humanus,* which transports the initiates to a post-nuclear

holocaust situation and forces them to make the most basic decisions about human worth.

- *Starpower,* a game about our economic system.[2]

We use these games for much the same reason that Hamlet staged a play in the midst of that great human tragedy. "The play's the thing wherein we catch the conscience of the king." Very often in the midst of a game it is possible to see conscience emerging, ethical passions being fueled, and humans becoming conscious of their condition. Most memorable is something that happened as we played *Starpower.*

The game creates a society with a three-tiered economic order, similar in many ways to the one in which we live. Two of the tiers are haves and have-nots. These find themselves in their economic predicaments usually because of circumstances over which they have little control. In the center is the great middle class. There are a few opportunities to move from one class to another, but these are meted out very sparingly by the Group-Overall-Director, G.O.D. Eventually, the two lower classes begin to rebel against their condition, angrily protesting against G.O.D. and threatening the wealthy ones, at which point G.O.D. turns over the task of making rules and setting limits to the haves, "who have obviously shown greater competence and worth." Shortly after this transfer of power the game ends in chaos.

But one night, just before the game came to its chaotic conclusion, an impassioned argument erupted among the have-nots who were sharply divided on how to remedy their plight. Some argued for anarchy, others for non-cooperation, others for compliance. Finally one voice rose above the rest. It belonged to a son of a single mother who managed to keep her family off the welfare rolls by holding down a marginal job. "Listen," he shouted, "those people are rich because they're smarter than we are. They deserve what they got. Just

136

play the game and don't complain." In the debriefing that followed we talked about his statements and he began to realize he was not predestined to poverty.

So often, learning about life comes by chance, not by design. One evening we sat in our room talking to poverty lawyers. We were supposed to be learning how they helped poor people, but the overriding question was, "How much do you guys earn?"

It was fairly obvious that these young attorneys had not come prepared to answer this question, even though they had promised "no holds barred, any questions can be asked." After a full five minutes of trying to avoid the issue ("Well, *most* lawyers earn . . . A person just out of law school earns . . . You should ask your parents that one, ha, ha!"), the air was getting so thick you could almost feel it. Finally, one of the lawyers broke the spell, said simply that he earned $20,000, confessed his embarrassment because his secretary, "who's more able than I am," made only $8,000, and recalled his own desire as a teenager to get his dad to divulge the family economics to him. Quite by surprise we began to realize that there is a mystery about money in our society, that there is more secrecy about fiscal affairs than sexual affairs, and that this mysterious power can control us, if we remain oblivious to it. Shortly after that meeting, I was told by several parents that, at their children's insistence, they had talked openly about their finances for the first time. To quote one parent, "It was actually liberating."

The unit on society ends with a mystery rite that we call "The Urban Adventure." In some ways this mystery rite is not much different from an urban retreat or even a visit to the city. In fact, some might wonder why we call it a mystery rite. The answer involves a strange type of logic:

- We call it a mystery rite so that it will become a mystery rite—the label helps the initiates to comprehend the mysterious ways of the city; they are not just visiting it but

137

are entering it; not just seeing it but feeling it; they come not as tourists, but as searchers.

- We also call it a mystery rite because it follows the rhythm of separation-transition-return; it helps us understand that which we ultimately can never understand. The city is not a set of problems to be solved, but a mystery to be lived.

The Urban Adventure begins, as do all the mystery rites, with an act of separation. We gather in the church parking lot, receive final instructions for the journey, say goodbye to parents, and drive off to the city. Any city will do. We generally go to New York.

Once we arrive in the city, we begin a series of activities, some to teach the techniques of urban living, some to touch upon its mysteries. The most profitable have been the "Urban Scavenger Hunt" and the "Nocturnal Urban Hike."

For the scavenger hunt, we divided ourselves into several groups. Each group is sent to different parts of the city with a walking map, a public transit map, enough money for subways or buses, and a list of instructions about where to go and what to find. Each list had ten specifics, such as:

1. Go to the headquarters of the United Nations. Bring back a U.N. stamp. Get information about the Security Council: the date of the next meeting and the primary item on the agenda.

2. At 475 Riverside Drive (Riverside and 120th Street) there is a large building. What is its name? List ten entities that have their headquarters there. Bring back the name of the commission that has its office on the seventh floor.

3. As you go through the city be conscious of homeless people. Be prepared to discuss their plight.

With the challenge laid out, the groups depart, each one accompanied by an adult who observes them and guarantees their safety, but who does not assist them in their search. In the course of the hunt, the initiates will learn firsthand much about city living.

138

The Nocturnal Urban Hike exposes them to the life of the city from another angle. We walk through the streets and see the street people. On every occasion, we have seen some of the human tragedy and depravity that contribute to the city scene. When we return to the warmth and safety of our accommodations—usually the basement of a church—we have much to talk about.

We do other things on our urban adventure, some of which are on the list of activities for any tourist. We visit the United Nations, go to the top of the Empire State Building or World Trade Center, ride the Staten Island Ferry, and take in a Broadway show. We also visit churches and talk with metropolitan ministers about the challenges to the church. The final act of the adventure is a sumptuous meal in a Chinese restaurant—eaten with chopsticks—followed by a ride home exhausted.

We are now ready to move on to more personal concerns.

The Unit on the Self

In olden days, the task of establishing a sense of self was aided by teaching persons the rules and roles of society and by assigning each person a particular function to fulfill. This process—socialization—began at birth and ended with death, but the turning point in character formation occurred during initiation.

Modern society is too complex for mere socialization. The rules change all the time. Many roles that once provided life with meaning and purpose have been cast aside in the name of progress. We need to assist persons in a more demanding and durable quest. We need to help them find a stable identity. Since the search for identity is the classic psycho-social task of adolescence, identity formation is a paramount concern of our initiation. It is our goal to assist the initiates in discovering

a unity of personality now felt by the individual and recognized by others as having consistency in time . . . a sense of inner self-sameness and continuity, to bind together the past, the present, and the future into a coherent whole.[3]

But the initiators cannot *give* an identity to the initiate. They can reflect only what they see, hint at possibilities, illumine some of the dark spots, and promise to support the adolescent as he or she seeks to achieve an identity.

> The word "achieve" is crucial here, for identity is not simply given by the society in which the adolescent lives; in many cases and in varying degrees, [one] must make [one's] own unique synthesis of the often incompatible models, identification and ideals offered by the society . . . The more incompatible the components from which the sense of identity must be built and the more uncertain the future for which one attempts to achieve identity, the more difficult the task becomes.[4]

> Character (the old term for identity) is not a set of doctrines or even a code of behavior, but an internal gyroscope, a self-activating, self-regulating, all-purpose inner control.[5]

Persons discover their sense of themselves in a multitude of ways: in isolation and in the company of others; by removing themselves from their everyday environment, and seeing themselves in historical and global perspectives; by expanding their "repertoire of self perceptions," imagining all types of possibilities for their lives; and also by selecting from among their possibilities that which seems most consistent with the emerging understanding of individual uniqueness. The search for identity can be exhausting. It can be lonely. It can be badly disrupted by overbearing judgment. It can be aborted forever by premature commitments to unrealistic and unrealizable possibilities.

To assist the initiates in their search, we help them to develop some skills in intentional living. We encourage them to explore the wider dimensions of their personality and to focus attention and energy on the most promising self-discoveries. We do this in the regular pattern of group meetings and in the increasingly comfortable community of fellow initiates. The structure of the initiation calls for two exercises and two mystery rites.

140

The first mystery rite involves a night spent in silence and solitude—a common motif in primitive cultures. We gather at the church late in the afternoon, each person equipped with a tent, a sleeping bag, and a minimal meal. We say goodbye to the parents and travel to a field where we work together to pitch all the tents, making sure that everyone knows how to get to the home base, where the advisors will spend the night. The young people are told to keep silence and also—if they wish—to keep a journal of their thoughts. They are encouraged to stay awake and watch the passing of the day to night and night to day. The primitives kept the novices awake for long periods of time in order to prove and enhance their maturity. "Not to sleep is not only to conquer physical fatigue, but is above all to show proof of will and spiritual strength; to remain awake is to be conscious, present in the world, responsible."[6]

In the morning, several hours after the break of dawn, the initiates are gathered one at a time and escorted to the opening of a large cave. When they descend to its depths, they are reunited as a group, and share the stories of their night over a hearty breakfast.

Anyone who spends much time with teenagers knows how little silence there is in their lives. The radio, TV, hi-fi, give a continuous cacophony of sound, which surely deadens their senses. One night of silence cannot pretend to reverse that trend, but it does provide them with a brief encounter with introspection, which later may prove a valuable memory. It also provides the model in which we want to learn to think and talk about ourselves. The two exercises—one traveling through the life cycle, the other attempting some life planning—work best when they grow out of silence and a quiet respect for human life.

The "Life Cycle Exercise" provides the young people a quick introduction to the different stages of life and makes them aware that life is passing—that *their* lives are passing. In order to accomplish this, we schedule seven or eight events in quick succession, beginning with birth, ending with death, and touching on life's turning points: childhood, adolescence, marriage, divorce, middle age, and old age. We encounter these stages in differing ways.

- For birth, we:
  See a movie on childbirth.
  Simulate the passage through the birth canal.
  Invite the youngest child in the congregation to visit us and have a doctor or nurse give the infant a physical exam.
- For childhood, we:
  See a movie on the pressures of childhood.
  Sit down with members of the fourth-grade church-school class and hear about their life firsthand.
  Talk with a child psychologist.
- For adolescence, we:
  Listen to one another.
  Invite a high school teacher to tell about the pressures of teaching adolescents.
  Discuss with a school administrator the inner workings of that institution which works with adolescents.
- For marriage, we:
  Have a panel discussion on different life styles—single, married, communal.
  Simulate a pre-marital counseling session.
  Walk through a marriage ceremony.
- For middle-age, we:
  Invite the parents to share their stories.
- For old age, we:
  Visit the elderly in several different settings—at home, in rest homes, in senior housing, in convalescent homes.
  We play a simulation game that portrays life's limits.
  We see movies.
- For death, we:
  Visit a funeral home.
  Attend a funeral.

Talk with terminally ill persons.

We do not attempt to schedule all these activities each year. It would take too long to move from birth to death, and we would never get the sense of life's passage. It takes about a month to move through the exercise, a total of seven or eight meetings.

Once we have completed our look at the life cycle, we move to the "Life-Planning Exercise." This is a simple, practical way to help persons become aware of who they are and who they wish to be, and then to lead them in setting life strategies so they can become all they wish to become.

The first step is to take stock of oneself, to be conscious of oneself as a unique historical entity interacting with other historical entities. Several exercises help in raising consciousness, as follows:

1. *Determine where you are on your own life line.* Take a paper. Draw a line. Put an X on one end and a second X on the other. One X signifies your birth; the other, your death. Mark the point where you are in relation to your birth and death.

2. *Analyze your name.* What is its etymology? Who else shares your name? Are there any biblical figures? or saints? What were their special qualities? Are you like them? Do you like your name?

3. *Assess yourself.* Finish the sentence "I am . . ." in ten different ways. When you have completed the ten, rank them, placing closest to you that which is most essential and furthest from you that which is most peripheral. Now introduce yourself to the others in the group and give one another feedback.

The next step includes some dreaming, trying to decide what you want to be or do. Once again, several exercises help to achieve this. The first one parallels the last mentioned exercise.

143

1. *Identify your dreams.* Finish the sentence "In my lifetime I want to be/or I want to do . . ." in ten different ways. Rank them in order of importance and share with the group.
2. *Write your obituary.* What would the local paper report on the day of your death?
3. *Name your heroes.* Include anyone at anytime whose life is a model for you.

The third part of the Life Planning Exercise is by far the most difficult. It includes setting strategies. This is difficult for adults, and much more so for adolescents. We attempt to give the initiates some skills by asking them to think of different units of time—the next year, the following four years, the following twenty—and to list activities they wish to pursue or goals they wish to achieve in each of those time frames. Those who can do this begin to set out some plans that will carry them into the next century. They must be reminded that such planning needs to be flexible, but they also need to be encouraged to plan. Too many lives lack direction and purpose because persons have not learned to live deliberately.

The final act of the unit on the self is a mystery rite. The "Masking Ritual" is a time-tested way to find one's identity. My first experience convinced me of its potential for self-discovery. Following a moving demonstration of some biblical personalities by a sculptor-actress, I volunteered to come forward and interact with some masks. First I studied them, becoming familiar with their lines and meanings. Then I chose one I wanted to know more fully. It was in the shape of a sun—a hard, cold, metal sun. When I put it in front of my face, I felt transformed. My personality was both concealed and revealed by the strange, yet familiar, representation that was, for the moment, connected to and identified with me. I was then invited to enter into dialogue with the audience, made up of caring friends or trusted acquaintances. In the midst of the ensuing dialogue, I became aware of a hidden part of me that was burning up and burning out behind the bright and shining face that the world saw.

This experience was so helpful to me that I began to read about customs surrounding masking in other cultures. I was surprised to see how widely the mask was used. The Greeks used the mask to portray different *personae*—characters—in their theater. The Romans picked up this custom and developed it further. The Latin word for mask is *larva,* which means not only mask but also ghost, mad or insane—a case of demoniacal possession. Larva is also "the immature form of animals characterized by metamorphosis" in the grub state before their transformation into a pupa or pupil. The parallel to young persons passing through initiation is self-evident. Marcus Aurelius used to advise, "carve your mask," meaning "develop your character, become yourself."[7]

In the Italian theater, masks were used to represent stock characters from different regions of Italy. The same characters appeared in numerous plays, living through a variety of experiences—gathering to themselves more and more life, a personal history, and a set of possibilities for the future. The mask was more important than the actor who wore it. That lifeless thing had attained a life of its own.

In Africa, both the making and the wearing of the mask are activities partaking of the holy. Consequently, they are protected with rites and taboos. Carving a mask frequently requires fasting, sexual abstinence, and a sacrifice to prevent the carver's becoming a victim of a power that his creation draws to itself. This is especially true with death masks, used throughout the world in a final attempt to unmask the essence of a person.[8]

Somehow, masking, by enabling humans to be other than what they normally are, allows them to be more of what they can be. The masks summon us to leave behind the conventions, the norms, the restrictions of the society, and enter the liminal world where we are given license to explore the wider dimensions of the self—both the heroic and the

145

diabolic. Think of the archetypal masked person. On one hand there are The Lone Ranger, Batman, Spiderman, Wonder Woman, and a panoply of superstars. On the other there are the highwayman, the masked bank robber, the terrorist, the Klu Klux Klansman. All are beyond the law. Some are above it; others are below it. The mask has concealed their mundane identity and revealed a hidden personality with far greater force.

Adolescents in our society often are caught in restrictive social norms caused by parental expectations, peer pressures, and rigid, self-imposed assumptions about who they ought to be. A masking ritual might free them temporarily from those restrictions and open them up to unexplored but more satisfying and promising aspects of themselves. That certainly was the case for some of the adolescents who were part of our initiation program.

The ritual we have designed has the familiar three-part movement: separation, transition, re-incorporation. The separation happens without much noise or activity. The initiates—who have fasted—gather and are told to relax, to forget whatever concerns they are carrying. They are then taken on a journey to a large, comfortable room. Actually it's the kindergarten room in our church. The room is filled with soft, romantic music. There are posters of heroes and heroines on the walls. On the tables are materials and tools for making masks. The instructions are given as simply as possible. "Create a mask for yourself."

Most initiates are able to do this, although they usually begin slowly and tentatively. If the group as a whole finds the assignment too difficult, or if a variation is desired, the adults may provide a selection of commercial masks. We sometimes offer a variety of hats, which can be used to top off the personalities.

When the masks are completed, the initiates are invited to present their creations by assuming the personality of the mask and allowing it to work its power of concealing-revealing.

146

The conversations through the mask have proven incredibly insightful. Over and again, the masked people speak to one another with a candor and a perceptivity that is frightening. For example:

● To a boy who had made a clown, I said: "Why did you make that?"

He replied: "Because it's the only way I can get attention. I'm the youngest of several children. My brothers and sisters are older, bigger, brighter, prettier. I have to become a clown so they'll notice me."

● To a boy who created a powerful mask with lightning bolts flashing out in all directions, but who then sat behind a partition so that no one could see him, I said: "Why are you sitting there?"

He said: "Because I'm afraid you'll see how powerful I am and make me do something."

● To a girl who created a classically pretty face out of a lace doily with red cheeks, beautiful eyes, long eyelashes—and a cigarette hanging out of the corner of her mouth, I said:

"Why did you stick that cigarette in your mouth?"

She said: "I don't know. I just did."

"Do you want me to tell you why?" asked a very able, attractive, authoritative boy in the group.

"I guess so."

"You stuck the cigarette in your mouth so you'd look tough and ugly. The fact is you can't accept the fact that you're really pretty. So when you make a pretty mask, you have to make it ugly, too. Better be careful, or you'll do the same thing with your life."

● To a boy who created two separate identities in one mask—identities that clearly reflected the confusion in his life about whether he was a "solid, all-American boy" or "a little devil," I said: "Do you know your mask has two images on it?"

"What do you mean?" he replied.

"Well, there's this square face right here. And there is also this wild-looking thing here."

"Wow! Why did I do that?"

"Why do you think?"

Statements such as those almost always strike a live nerve because we perceive not only the mask but the person behind the mask. The mask helps to focus the issues of a person's life. The conversations with the masks are a bit unreal and a bit too real.

When the conversation seems to have run its course, we begin the process of re-incorporation. We take off the masks and talk to one another face to face. We try to separate reality from unreality. We make every effort to reintegrate—to themselves and to the group—those who went furthest with their masks. Then, as is the custom in rites of passage, we conclude with a meal. This time it's sundaes. The material for the masks is swept aside, and on the same tables are set gallons of ice cream, hot fudge and butterscotch, peanuts and cherries, and lots of whipped cream. We all prepare our sugary creations and eat them.

It must be said that not all these rituals or exercises work. And none of them ever occurs exactly as envisioned. On some occasions, the mood of the group is wrong. At other times, there are more pressing agendas from the outside world. Sometimes the level of expectation from the advisors is unrealistic, and frustration and failure are the end results. But the effort is worth it. There are many moments when genuine insight occurs. Furthermore, the entire process is ordered in such a way that minimal learnings in one part can precipitate major breakthroughs in another.

"The Masking Ritual," quite frankly, is one of the more difficult and risky. Sometimes the group is unable to relax and become playful enough to do serious work. But even if the experience does not meet expectations, there are little lessons gleaned from the experience, which help to inform the subsequent experience of the group. More important, they provide valuable information to the initiates as they carry on the quests for identity.

The Unit on Sexuality

In our initiation, the unit on sexuality is now the third unit in the sequence. It was once the second, but the initiates were not yet comfortable enough with one another to share the dark secrets surrounding sexuality. It was also the last unit for a short period, but I decided that it was not wise to conclude with sexuality, for fear it might be seen either as the last word or as an afterthought. Our sexuality is a good and valuable part of life, but it is neither our damnation nor our salvation.

When I prepare for the unit on sexuality, I struggle with that fear. Humans fault on their basic humanity when they expect too much or too little from their sexuality. People—most notably young people—can destroy themselves with inappropriate, premature intimacies. But an intimate relationship can also provide the warmth and tenderness for genuine self-sharing and self-growth. It is often hard to distinguish between a destructive and a constructive relationship until too late. But we communicate sexually about sexuality in all that we do. So perhaps it's best to raise our feelings to consciousness and share them openly, in a patterned and structured environment that lets us explore the depths without being overwhelmed by them.

The program for this unit on sexuality is based on the following assumptions.

- Sexuality is a gift of God, who made us male and female, so we could procreate, and communicate, and just plain enjoy one another. Our sexuality is a powerful force that would surge out of control if we did not accept some limitations on its expression.
- Monogamy is a desirable state in which one man and one woman covenant to love and cherish each other all the days

149

of their life. My experience is that—contrary to many widely held beliefs—the human psyche cannot handle multiple intimacies without some damage. We buy into second and third intimate relationships only at a cost to the first relationship. Usually there is a loss of self-confidence and mutuality when it becomes clear that one partner is sharing the signs of deepest intimacy with still another. Sometimes the debts that are accumulated during experimentation with the so-called "new freedom" do not become evident until many years later, when it becomes obvious that basic trust has eroded away.

- Desirable as monogamy is, however, some marriages should be legally dissolved. I am willing to counsel divorce, if such seems the necessary course.

- Though I do not fully comprehend the phenomenon of homosexuality, I recognize it as a way of life for many persons who know that there is no simple or sure way to alter their sexual preference. Persons of homosexual preference deserve not only the civil rights due any one, but also some socially and ecclesiastically accepted way to covenant with another human in a relationship of respect and tenderness.

- A double standard that prescribes different modes of behavior for the two sexes is wrong. Furthermore, the old sex-ethic, with its single, negative principle—no pre-marital sexual intercourse—is outmoded. It must be replaced by a more affirmative posture in which we seek to discover means of sexual expression—in and out of marriage, among friends and with intimates—that include signals of affection and signs of deepest intimacy. We can expand our range of sexual expression as we limit sexual intercourse to one or a very few relationships.

- My concern with adolescents is more with premature intimacy than with pre-marital intercourse. This does not mean that I endorse promiscuity. I will tell any adolescent who asks that under no circumstances do I believe it would

150

be wise or healthy for persons in their early teens to engage in sexual intercourse. The excitement of the moment will be forgotten long before the damage has been repaired—if it ever gets repaired.

Others, including those who share the task of guiding our initiates, may differ with me. That is their right in this pluralistic society. It is essential, however, for the advisors to take some time to air different points of view, and perhaps even to talk with parents about their concerns. Since we are not trying to impose an ethical system on the initiates, it is good to know the ethical systems that order our own lives, and thereby protect against their unwitting imposition.

Since we are not trying to impose a system of values, it might help to explain what we are trying to accomplish in this unit on sexuality. We are trying to impart knowledge and dispel myths. We are trying to teach a language and tell out our own stories, so that the initiates can have some of the ingredients they will need to live out their unique life stories. We are trying to create a community where they can share confusion and hurts, where they can ask questions and feel supported in their search for answers. We are, to some extent, trying to teach techniques for intimacy, but more important, we are trying to sensitize them to the deeper issues of what it means to be female and male. We are offering to stand with them and protect them as they explore their mixed feelings about sexual identity, as they move to resolve the ambivalence and strike out on the road of manhood or womanhood.

The unit begins with a mystery rite. The initiates are brought to the church parking lot—ideally on a bitter cold night and the initiates having eaten little or nothing during the day. As they stand shivering in the parking lot they are told that they are going on a journey back to the time of creation. They need not be afraid, but they must listen carefully and follow directions. They are then blindfolded, ushered to a

151

van, and delivered by a circuitous route to a mystical building. The adult initiators have warmed a room with a crackling fire and have scattered soft mattresses around the room.

When the van arrives, bullroarers are whirled, thunders are sounded, human hoots and shrieks begin. The initiates are escorted—one at a time—to their mattresses. They are still blindfolded, but they can hear the sounds of chaos all around them.

Then the quiet voice of the storyteller emerges:

> In the beginning . . . in the beginning . . . in the beginning, *God*.

The thunders cease, the chaos subsides, and the initiates are told to relax, to quiet themselves, to become like blobs of clay, just lying there waiting to be created.

> In the beginning, the earth was without form and void . . . [thunders begin slowly and move quickly to tumultuous crashing] . . . and darkness was upon the face of the deep . . . and the Spirit of God was moving upon the waters. [the bullroarers begin to whirl and the noise becomes deafening.] and God shouted LET THERE BE LIGHT . . . [sudden silence] . . . and there was light. And God saw the light was good; and God separated it from the darkness. God called the light Day, and the darkness he called Night. And there was evening, and there was morning, one day.

In the silence that follows that first day of creation the Initiates are told to rest, to relax, to become inanimate. They remain in that lifeless state as the next days of creation are quickly recounted until we arrive at the sixth day.

> And God came and looked around and looked at you. God saw you, a blob of clay without form—no feet. Can you feel your feet? Then tighten the muscles. Tighter! Now drop them off! [Same with calves, kneebone, and other body parts.] And you feel God looking at you. And hear God say, "Let us create human-beings. Let us make some male and female . . . " And you imagine . . . imagine—get an image, a picture in your

mind's eye—that you are to be female. Imagine yourself in your mother's womb, gradually taking form . . . the form of a human . . . the form of a female. Imagine coming down the birth canal and being born. . . . Feel yourself as an infant, a little baby girl at your mother's breast. . . . Feel yourself feeling yourself. . . . Does it feel good? . . . Then become a two-year old girl running around the house, playing with those special toys. . . . become five . . . a big five-year old, walking down the street on the way to your first day at school. . . . How does it feel to go to school? Now become twelve, almost a teenager, very conscious of boys, very conscious of yourself. Feel yourself growing to be a woman . . . let your body take shape . . . start having periods . . . how does it feel? Allow yourself to graduate from high school. . . . Where does your life go? to college? to a first job? to marriage? Imagine yourself a young woman in college . . . or starting a job and bringing home your first paycheck . . . or getting married. Leave your parents' home for a dorm, apartment, first house. How does it feel to be on your own? Now you marry . . . decide to have a family. Become pregnant . . . feel the body growing in your body . . . feel the incredible joy of giving birth . . . feel the baby nursing at your breast. Watch your child grow to teenage, and feel yourself grow older. . . . Where does your life go as your child leaves home for college, job, or marriage? Do you get a job, continue a career, stay home? How does it feel to be a middle-aged woman? Grow older still . . . become an old woman, wise with the experience of a lifetime, looking back at your life . . . having grandchildren . . . losing your husband to illness. Finally, let yourself die . . . die . . . and turn slowly but surely back to dust . . . a blob of clay . . . relaxed, peaceful, lifeless clay.

As you lie there, totally relaxed, you sense God looking at you once again. And you imagine that you are to be born male . . .

The life cycle starts again. This time the suggestions guide them through the masculine existence. When they have grown old and died and return to dust, they are ready to be born again.

> Now you feel God coming to you again, coming close, going away . . . coming close . . . going away . . . coming very close . . . coming *so* close . . . bending down to blow the breath of life into your nostrils and whisper the secret of your sexuality into your ear.

And with that an adult midwife kneels over each adolescent and whispers in his or her ear, "John, you shall be born male." or "Mary, you shall be born female." The midwife then removes the blindfold and raises the new-born to life. The moment is always awe-inspiring. For a while we can do nothing but sit in silence as the benediction is said once again.

> And God made us male and female. And God saw what he had made, and behold it was very good, *very good*. Amen. Amen. Amen.

Slowly the power of the mystery rite eases. The initiates are brought one at a time to the fire, where we eat pizza and drink soda, sit and talk, and marvel anew at our creation as male and female.

As always, conversation is important. This is particularly true with the sexuality rite. I remember one young man who confessed that, though he tried hard to stay with the whole fantasy trip, there was one point when he could not relate. "I just couldn't be an old woman. It seemed so awful."

"Oh, it's not so bad," said a voice out of the darkness. The voice was that of a seventy-year-old church member who was part of the team of adult initiators. She was eager to tell the story of her life and would have taken the boy off for private conversation had not the full group wanted to hear it.

Sometimes the fantasy trip leads an initiate to surprising places within himself or herself. "I couldn't believe it," said a young woman, the daughter of two of the most liberated people in our church. "Not only did I wear frilly dresses all through my childhood (in the fantasy), but the day I got my first paycheck I walked into the house, handed it to my husband, who thanked me, and kept it. But when my husband

154

came home with his, he just put it in his pocket." With that we discussed how married couples can share, not only paychecks, but respect, gratitude, and authority.

Sometimes the sexuality rite takes initiates all the way back to the beginning and allows them to approach their sexuality in radically new ways:

> I can't believe what happened to me. I relaxed totally. My whole being was spinning and spinning in chaos. Then I went completely through life as a female and a male. But then the most amazing thing happened. When God kept coming close and going away, I felt this strange thing building within me. And then when God came and whispered that I was to be a female, it was as if I was born again. When God lowered my blindfold I saw myself in new ways. It's almost as if tonight I was born as a woman.

Following the classic forms, the sexuality rite takes the initiates back to the time before time and enables them to participate in the creation of themselves as sexual beings. It opens them up to the totality of their inherent bi-sexuality and then channels them to paths that are appropriate to them. One can never be sure where the sexuality rite will lead. It is crucially important, therefore, that the masters of the initiation be conscious of the concerns and the levels of maturity that become evident in the course of the evening.

These concerns and levels of maturity should inform your development of the unit on sexuality. You need to speak to issues in the initiates' lives, not to those in yours. Beware of subtle pressures, such as talking about sexual practices in ways that make the initiates feel inadequate if not presently involved. Know that individual experiences vary. For some adolescents, dating has not yet begun and may never; for others, intercourse is common by junior high. Consequently some adolescents will be wondering how to get up the courage or to find the right words to ask a classmate out for the Saturday night dance, while others will be worried that they

155

are not regularly achieving orgasm and fearful that something is basically wrong with them. Remember, even the most comprehensive initiations in primitive societies did not try to provide all the knowledge known to adults. They sought only to provide the minimal knowledge necessary to enter the next stage of life. Jesus told his disciples, "I have much more I could tell you but you cannot hear it now" (John 16:12, author's paraphrase).

It is difficult to learn what the initiates already know about sexuality. Adolescents like to appear knowledgeable. They are afraid to show their ignorance. They are particularly afraid to show their ignorance to members of the opposite sex.

Therefore, we follow the mystery rite with an anatomy lesson. In that session—or sessions—a doctor who is part of the congregation explains the functioning of the male and female sex organs, including their development from birth, through puberty, into adulthood. We explain conception and contraception. We discuss abortion—both the procedures and the agonies of making the decision regarding abortion. We explain the experience of sexual excitement. We introduce the initiates to the experience of pleasuring another. We invite and answer all questions.

We then divide into single-sex groups for several sessions during which we ask questions and offer answers. To stimulate the discussion we have developed a lengthy vocabulary list. It includes street language and medical language. It has diagrams related to it. The initiates are expected to learn these terms. To deepen the conversation we also have a list of typical questions asked by boys and girls as they pass through adolescence. Most important, we have the questions from the lives of the initiates.[9]

After these sessions, we meet as a whole group to share some of the concerns and questions that arose in the single-sex groups. By now the initiates have practiced the language and are considerably less awkward with one

156

another. They are ready to meet visitors with varying life styles. Most important to the initiates, they are ready to talk to their peers about themselves.

This unit on sexuality follows the model laid out by the primitives. After we open up a range of considerations for the initiates, we focus on the most personal concerns. We talk about our own bodies—what we like and dislike about them. The initiates share their impressions of one another, and they try to answer the questions that plague us all: "What do men want from women? What do women want from men?" Or, by now, "What do *you* want from *me?*"

> The answers to those questions are often surprising. "Until tonight," remarked one attractive young woman, "I just assumed boys wanted to go all the way with you. And if you won't do it, they won't ask you out again. But I believe you guys when you say you'd rather just date. . . . But how can I tell someone outside the group that I don't want to get serious?

It is obvious that this question comes from the center of her life. The answer must come from the center of yours.

> You'll have to ask and answer that question all your life. How, when you are sexually attractive and attracted, can you tell someone you don't want to get intimate? Your answer must be tactful, yet as direct as is needed. What I say is . . . "Look, I like you. I find you attractive, but I do not want to be any more intimate with you than we are now. I hope we can remain close."

This is the way sexuality education makes sense. We speak as candidly as possible. When we don't know the answers, we admit our lack of knowledge and promise to search for the answers. When we are giving personal opinions, we own them as such. Throughout, we try to create an environment where adolescent confusion can move toward clarity, where teenage anxieties can yield to a capacity to be at ease with one's sexuality, where the God-given gift that made us male and

157

female can be received and relished by emerging men and women.

The Unit on Spirituality

Learning about spirituality—both the human spirit and the Holy Spirit—takes place throughout this entire venture. From the very first event, we are conscious of the religious component in all we do.

- The unit on society is shaped out of the Christian ethic: a concern for the poor and oppressed, a determination that we as Christians must be wise as serpents and innocent as doves, and a desire to have these emerging adults see the social implications of our gospel of love.

- In a similar manner, the unit on the self teaches both self-propriety and the selflessness that is central to our faith.

- And the unit on sexuality is offered with the hope that the initiates will come to know the goodness of their sexuality, even as they come to know its power and danger.

Throughout the experience, initiates worship regularly with the congregation. Most of them sing in the choir, thereby learning some fundamental disciplines of religious life. I will never forget the time two of the Initiates surprised me with the news that they were "very religious." The two happened to play short stop and second base on the high school baseball team. I picked them up after a game to take them to a retreat. As we rode we talked about baseball, high school, cars, girls, and finally religion: heaven and hell, faith and doubt, prayer and miracles. It was the type of conversation every minister fantasizes about! They were genuinely interested—eager to hear my thoughts and even more eager to share theirs.

When they began asking about being "born again," I decided I needed to know more about the religious climate in the high school. "Do you have any friends who are very religious, like Jehovah's Witnesses or charismatics?" After a moment of silence, a voice came from the back seat. "When I

158

think about it, Danny and I are the most religious kids I know." I quickly looked in the rear view mirror to make sure those words came from the short stop I had picked up at the baseball field a few hours ago. They did. And he continued. "I mean, we're the only ones who go to church and actually like it. Some others may go, but they hate it. But we like it. And everyone knows we like it. So I guess that makes us religious."

As I drove on I wondered about his statement. At first I was astounded. I just had not considered these initiates religious. But as I thought, I could see how this faith made them religious in the original meaning of that word. "Religion" comes from the Latin root *ligare,* which means "to bind or hold together." The word ligament comes from the same Latin root. To be religious, therefore, means "to bind or hold together again." In that sense of the word, the short-stop and his friend were deeply religious. They were using religious disciplines and their emerging faith to hold them together through the turbulence of adolescence.

As I thought further, I was also impressed by their evangelistic style. "We go to church and actually like it. Everyone knows we like it." They were sharing the good news in a way that seemed consistent with their age and character. Maybe someday their faith would mature to the point where they could "preach Christ crucified."

The initiation experience should help that day to come. Therefore, in addition to considering religious concerns throughout the two-year journey, we reserve a substantial period of time for a unit on spirituality.

The unit begins with a mystery rite for Ash Wednesday, the first day of Lent. We have designed "A Service of Penitence Separating the Candidates from the Church." It is an old service for the Christian church, but a new service for our congregation. Consequently, we provide a lengthy introduction to the service, including a set of instructions written by a twelfth-century scholar, Gratian:

159

On the first day of Lent the penitents were to present themselves before the Bishop, clothed with sack-cloth, with naked feet, and eyes turned to the ground; and this was to be done in the presence of the principal of the Clergy of the Diocese, who were to judge of the sincerity of the repentance. These introduced them to the church where the Bishop, all in tears, and the rest of the Clergy, repeated the 7 penitential psalms . . . then, with mournful sighs declared to them, that as Adam was thrown out of Paradise, so they will be thrown out of the Church. Then the Bishop commanded the officers to turn them from the Church doors.[10]

The service begins with silence, followed by a Lenten hymn, scripture readings, and reflection on the lessons. The initiates are then called forward for an examination.

Examination of the Penitents
Leader: Do you know, oh child, that from dust you have come and to dust you shall return?
Penitents: I do.
Leader: Do you know that you are a child of Adam, who sinned against the Lord, God Almighty, in thought, word and deed, and are unworthy of His gracious care?
Penitents: I do.
Leader: Then prostrate yourselves before our God in an act of humble submission.

As they lie on the cold floor, the 51st Psalm is said and sung over them. "Create in me a clean heart, O Lord, and renew a right spirit within me . . ." They are then marked with ashes and expelled from the church.

As Adam has sinned, so have you.
As Adam was thrown out of paradise,
so must you be thrown out of the church, to observe the forty days of holy Lent by self examination and repentance; by prayer; fasting; and self-denial; by reading and meditating upon God's word. And, to serve as the constant reminder that you are dust and to dust you shall return, I now mark you with the ashes of an offence. _____ Dust you are and to dust you shall return. You go with our prayers.

As they go, the congregation offers an ancient prayer on their behalf:

> O God, who art justly angry, and dost mercifully pardon, accept the tears of thy afflicted people and graciously turn away thy wrathful indignation, which they righteously deserve. Grant unto us, we beseech thee, O Lord, so to commence and protect our Christian warfare by holy fasts, that we who are about to fight against spiritual wickedness may be fortified by the aid of continence. Through Jesus Christ our Lord.
>
> —Sarum Missal (1526)

The service ends with a powerful but eerie Lenten hymn, one that is credited to St. Andrew of Crete (660-732) and may well have been sung for hundreds of years at services of penitence separating the candidates from the Church.

> Christian, dost thou see them On the holy ground
> How the powers of darkness Compass them around?
> Christian, up and smile then, Counting gain but loss,
> In the strength that cometh, By the holy cross.
>
> Christian, dost thou feel them, How they work within,
> Striving, tempting, luring, Goading into sin?
> Christian, never tremble, Never be downcast;
> Gird thee for the battle, watch and pray and fast.[11]

The Ash Wednesday Service is strange. But when it is over both the initiates and the congregation are ready for Lent—a period of intensification of study and prayer.

The period is particularly intense for the initiates. We have two goals: to impart basic knowledge about the faith and to awaken them to a life of faithfulness. Each of the following seven sub-units is designed to realize both goals.

1. *The Scriptures—Their Origin and Shape.*

We are persuaded that the initiates are mature enough to do some serious study of the Bible, but they first need some basic information about the development and variety of the scriptures.

- We introduce them to the documentary theory and assign them the task of reconciling the conflicting statements in the story of Noah's Ark.
- We use the Psalms as a worship book.
- We read the Prophets as inspiration.
- In turning to the New Testament we compare sections of the Synoptic Gospels—Matthew, Mark, and Luke—and identify the different sources behind them.
- We read Paul's letters as letters and see the Apocalypse as inspiration to a persecuted church.

We conclude this sub-unit with a review of the structure of the Bible, verifying that the initiates know the difference between the Wisdom Literature and the Pentateuch, the Gospels and the Epistles, the Apocrypha and the canon.[12]

2. *The Old Testament.*

We approach the Hebrew scriptures with our two-fold concern—to know about the faith and to sense the powerful religious experience in human life.

To accomplish the first, we distribute a list of terms that the initiates must identify, arrange in chronological order, and utilize in recounting the history of the People of Israel. To give them some sense of the religious experience, we create Bible sculptures.

Bible sculpture is an adaptation of a therapeutic technique called family sculpture, often used to portray the inner dynamics of a family from the differing perspectives of its members. In both experiences an "artist" is chosen to create a moving sculpture that expresses his or her perspective. In Bible sculpture, the artist selects a story, shares the vision that is formed in his or her mind's eye, introduces the particulars of that image—the background, the scene, the participants, the action—sets the stage, enlists the actors, gives them directions, and then steps back to let it come alive. The creating of the sculpture is immediately followed by

162

discussion. What did the audience see? What did the actors experience? Was the artist's vision realized?

It is astonishing how fully the initiates can enter into the scriptures and live them. One of their favorite sculptures depicts "the binding of Isaac." They know the anguish of father Abraham as he prepares to sacrifice his son—his only son, the one he loves. They experience the horror of Isaac as he confronts his own holocaust. They feel the helplessness of Sarah, left at home as her husband takes her son away. They empathize with the lowly servants who do what they are told, even when it seems all wrong. They even wonder with God about how to act in human history. In brief, they live the story. It becomes part of their life.

3. *The New Testament.*

The same two-fold goal is pursued as in the Old Testament. On one hand the initiates are expected to know about Jesus' life. They are encouraged to enter his life and let his life enter theirs. To accomplish this we create Bible sculptures, we see movies, and—as Holy Week approaches—we observe a time-honored tradition of reading the Passion from the Gospel of Mark. For some unknown reason, that experience is one of the turning points in the initiation. The adolescents find themselves strangely moved.

Once, when we had finished the reading, a heavy silence fell over the group. Finally one boy broke the silence. "Wow. I feel funny. I feel different. Hearing that story changed me."

A moment later, a girl admitted that she had never really listened before, but now she too felt different. Soon after, a third initiate suggested that this whole conversation was "a bit weird. It's just a story, isn't it? Why are you getting so worked up?"

As they talked among themselves, I remembered those times in my life when I first began to hear the Word. I shared those memories as best I could, and then we talked about the variety of religious experiences. The initiates were coming closer to the day when the faith of our fathers could be passed on to them—and through them to their children. They were coming closer to the day when they could own the faith.

4. *Church History.*

In this sub-unit, the initiates study the terms, identify the personalities, and learn the story of our faith for two thousand years. As we move to the present, we focus our attention more narrowly on our particular heritage—Congregationalism and the United Church of Christ. We conclude by studying our local congregation, its history and polity.

5. *The World's Other Religions.*

Having surveyed the Judeo-Christian tradition from Abraham to the present, we take a cursory look at other expressions of faith. We see films, learn history, meet believers of Islam, Buddhism, and Hinduism, and—if possible—attend their worship.

6. *The Creeds of the Church.*

"Every new generation of Christians needs to formulate what it believes and to draw up its articles of faith in contemporary terms, which all may understand."[13] So begins an excellent little book on words of faith. In order to help this generation with that task, we introduce them to the creeds of earlier generations. We study the ecclesiastical language, the trinitarian structure, and the controversies behind the creeds. Then we come to the present, meeting with selected adults from the congregation. Some are "born again" college students. Some are young parents who came to First Church to find a church school for their children and are finding a faith for themselves. Some are older church members whose loyalty to the institution was inherited from parents and grandparents. These are the people of faith. These are the priests in the priesthood of all believers. They have become the experts on their own religious lives. They have important faith stories for the initiates to hear.

But the initiates are meant to be more than hearers of someone else's faith. They need to form their own and share it.

7. *The Initiate's Faith.*

Two years ago, when the initiates were mere P.I.G.s, they sat and listened as emerging adults presented statements of the faith. From then on they have known that they too would someday stand in that line of believers. Now they prepare a rough draft, and then go off for a mystery rite.

We call this rite the "Wilderness Experience." The rite is designed to give the group time to integrate all that they have experienced over the last two years. They address themselves fully to the task of forming and sharing their faith.

The Wilderness Experience begins—as do the other mystery rites—with an act of separation. The parents bring the novices to the church parking lot with all the material for a few days in the wilds. They have tents, sleeping bags, cooking utensils, food, and backpacks. They also have first drafts of their statements of faith. During the time in the wilderness— as they climb mountains and conquer white water, and as they create a place to sleep and prepare food to eat—they will share their faith with one another.

Over the years, I have seen the initiates struggle to express their faith. Each time I have rejoiced. I have vague but unhappy memories of my own confirmation, when I dutifully parrotted back rehearsed affirmations to unanalyzed questions. I have less vague and even more unhappy memories of confirmations at which *I* was the officiant. Before me stood confirmands who were hearing words they did not really comprehend, but to which they nevertheless gave their consent. In those days, it often seemed that the truly thoughtful adolescents sat with the congregation and watched as their classmates said "I do." For many the most affirmative act was to say "no" to confirmation.

With the initiation groups, this does not happen. We have been together too long and have grown too close. There is no way that we could revert suddenly to ecclesiastical roles for the sake of a ceremony. There was no way that I or any other adult could formulate a faith to which they would give their approval. The adults, following the example given by Jesus at the Last Supper, were about ready to leave the initiates.

> I will tell you the truth: it is for your good that I am leaving you. If I do not go, your Advocate will not come, whereas if I go, I will send him to you. . . . There is still much I could say to you, but the burden would be too great for you now. However, when he comes who is the Spirit of Truth, he will guide you into all truth . . . and he will make known to you the things that are coming (John 16:7, 12–13 NEB).

The adults must leave so that the initiates can take these steps to the faith on their own. If the father writes the Bar Mitzvah sermon, the son remains the son of the father; he never becomes a son of the law. If the adults write the adolescents' statements of faith, their faith is blocked from growing to mature adulthood. They must meet the challenge on their own.

To persuade the initiates that they are equal to this spiritual challenge, the mystery rite presents them with a physical test. When we go to the wilderness, we set out objectives that appear to be beyond the individuals' capacities. We climb mountains that are too high. We canoe through white water that is too dangerous. We suffer insufferable black flies. We endure endless rains. We even have snowshoed in unbearable cold.

At all times, the adults try to guide the initiates up to the extent of their abilities. We make every effort to guarantee personal safety, but we also are determined to get the young persons to stretch beyond their limits, to break through to new competencies, to grow. Fortunately we have never had a serious injury, though we have had some minor scratches and bruises. But on almost all experiences we have arrived at a point at which the initiates—singly or as a group—have felt as if they could go no further. Since that point always occurs when we are miles from civilization, they have no choice but to summon up willpower they did not know they had, to call upon reserves of strength they never dreamed about, and, by sheer willpower, to do the impossible.

That is a great experience! It's the stuff that makes heroes. Yet, too many young people never hear the challenge to surpass themselves. All they hear are the complaints. "In the old days it was never this easy."

Now those complaints are a thing of the past. So are the complaints that they cannot go a step farther. For all have gone many steps further than they thought they could. With this heightening sense of themselves, they share their faith, first with one another, and then with the congregation.

There is no meal as we drive home from the Wilderness Experience. The act of incorporation for this mystery rite occurs the next night at the initiation banquet, attended by parents, officers and members of the congregation, the Graduates, Initiates, and the PIGs, who now stand in awe of the initiates. With appropriate fear and trembling, the soon-to-be-born adults approach the microphone, read their statements of faith, and sit to entertain questions and comments from the church members. The PIGs just sit in silence.

This event is always a victory. It is not easy to stand in front of a large group and give an account of your faith. Yet it is an important part of the heritage we share. To this day, our Jewish brothers and sisters stand before the congregation on the occasion of the Bar Mitzvah, read the Torah in unvoweled Hebrew, and explain the meaning of the text in their own words. Likewise, our Pentecostal and evangelical brothers and sisters are accepted by the congregation when they stand to tell their conversion experience in their own words. So, now, our initiates tell us of their faith, using their own words and ideas.

The statements of faith are as varied as the gifts and life experiences of the initiates. Some speak the language of the church; others, the language of science; still others, the language of science fiction. But the most memorable statements of all use the language of *life*.

I will never forget the simple eloquence of a girl who had

167

been in an automobile accident on Christmas Day five years earlier. She lay unconscious and paralyzed for months, spoke her first words sometime late in the spring, spent years in the hospital, worked hard enough and healed fully enough to be a loyal and able member of the Initiation Group. She stood to offer us her faith. "I believe in God the Creator. He has done wonderful things for me in the past and I believe he will do the same for me in the future." Then she sat down. She had said it all.

By now, the Initiation Group has pretty much done it all. One thing alone remains. And what a mighty thing it is.

The Rite of Incorporation

Do you remember the statement about the norm of Christian baptism? "Baptism is solemn sacramental initiation done especially at the paschal vigil and preceded by a catechumenate of serious intent and considerable duration."[14] The full initiation should include (1) an act of separation from the world of childhood; (2) a period of training and testing; and (3) an act of incorporation. This final act in turn should include (a) baptism, (b) confirmation—with any of several liturgical acts: laying on of hands, signing with the cross, anointing, commissioning, extending the right hand of fellowship, owning the covenant—and (c) a meal of bread and wine.

I am mystified by the manner in which our congregation is wedded to that norm, even though our practices would seem to frustrate the relationship at almost every point. Most initiates are already baptized, because we baptize infants. Most have taken communion for years, because we have not "fenced the table" in any way. And we would never dream of adding initiation to our already full Easter worship.

But—you may remember—a norm does not require that it be followed in every particular.

A norm has nothing to do with how many times a thing is done, but has everything to do with the standard according to how a thing is done. So long as the norm is in place both in practice and in the awareness of those who are engaged in it, the situation is capable of being judged 'normal' even though the norm may be departed from to some extent, even frequently, due to exigencies of time, place, pastoral considerations, physical inabilities, or whatever.[15]

Pastoral considerations cause me to think it both unwise and unnecessary to advise against infant baptism. It is the custom in our church. The custom bears witness to one of the great truths of our faith: namely, that the gift of God's love is freely given; we do not have to earn it. I confess that pastoral considerations might cause me to dissuade—but certainly not to prohibit—a pre-adolescent from seeking baptism. Furthermore, pastoral consideration, coupled with theological beliefs and ecumenical concerns, preclude the re-baptism of anyone. Consequently, most Initiates will miss baptism at their initiation.

But not all. Because of an influx of persons from other traditions—some of which practice believer's baptism—and because of changing attitudes in our culture whereby increasing numbers of parents are choosing to withhold baptism from infants, there are always one or more initiates who will be baptized at their initiation.

Originally there was a shyness about adult baptism, and therefore, the first initiate baptism was private. Only the parents and fellow initiates were present. By the second initiation, that shyness had eased; the baptism was part of the Sunday morning service. Prior to the third baptism, we discussed the rite of the third century church and moved the baptism closer to the center of the initiation. Now—and for the foreseeable future—the sacrament of baptism is placed at the heart of our celebration, rooting our experience in the life, death, and resurrection of Jesus Christ.

In a similar manner, pastoral considerations cause me to

169

think it unwise to alter our practice of inviting children to partake of the Lord's Supper. They learn about the mysteries in both children's worship and church school. They are included in many aspects of the congregation's life. To bar the children from the table would be to compromise their sense of belonging.

But even with regard to communion there is a way to make the initiation meal special. Pastoral considerations of long standing have led this particular congregation to serve bread and grape juice. On Pentecost, when we initiate young adults, we offer wine.

The decision to schedule our initiation for Pentecost was an easy one. That holiday is the traditional time for confirmation in both Judaism and Christianity. To the Jews, Pentecost is the Festival of Weeks, marking the gift of the Torah to Moses on Mt. Sinai. To Christians, Pentecost is fifty days after Easter, marking the gift of the Holy Spirit to the first disciples. To First Church in Middletown, every other Pentecost is the Day of Initiation.

The day begins early, at least for the initiates. They gather in their room in the basement. Much has happened in that space, and there is a certain sadness as they realize that this is the last time they will be together in that room. Soon the room will belong to the present P.I.G.s. Soon the initiates will be graduates, taking their part along with the other adults in the church and society. There is something sad about growing up. We cannot deny it. We do not try. We express it in our worship, along with the joy of accomplishment that we celebrate.

Before the service, the initiates have a few final moments to talk with the guides before they are taken on one last journey. They walk through the darkness of the church basement to a trap door. As they pass into the light, they are greeted by—of all things—their parents, who have the bittersweet assignment of escorting them to the sanctuary. They enter as the congregation pours out one of the great hymns that expresses the continuity of our faith from age to age. They take their seats with the congregation as the last mystery rite unfolds.

After a general confession, scripture reading, and brief meditation we move to the heart of the ritual:

1. *The Separation from the Parents*

All over the sanctuary, parents stand with their children, then walk down the aisle to a point where one of the initiators intercepts them and instructs the parents to bid their children goodbye for the final time. The parents then express themselves in whatever manner seems fitting. The moment is very powerful. So is the next one. The parents return to their now emptied pews. Their children present themselves for examination.

2. *The Sacrament of Baptism*

Led by those of their company not yet baptized, the initiates move *en masse* to the baptismal font. The age-old questions about Jesus Christ as Lord and Savior are asked. The candidates for baptism answer with sufficient entry-level knowledge to give integrity to their confession. Those who have shared the journey, and who consequently know much more about death and rebirth, join them in answering—almost in the manner of godparents or sponsors. The congregation adds its voice of affirmation and the sacrament is performed. All of us experience or re-experience the one baptism that we share.

3. *The Initiation-Confirmation-Incorporation Questions*

With our faith declared through singing, the initiates move from the baptismal font to face the congregation. They hear the questions dealing with three separate but related matters:

1. Initiation to adulthood.
2. Confirmation of faith.
3. Admission to adult membership in the congregation.

Our questions are simple; their meaning is clear.

- Will you, with God's help, assume the rights and responsibilities of adulthood in relation to the society, the church, and your self?

- Will you, with God's help, reaffirm your faith in Jesus Christ as our Lord and Savior?
- Will you, with God's help, promise to become a responsible member of this congregation, walking with us and our God in Christian fellowship and service?

The answer in each case is, "I will," which has a special significance. To *will* something is an act of selfhood. It means to commit oneself to live with the vicissitudes of the future in such a way that one can influence the future in accordance with one's intention—one's will.

4. *Questions of the Congregation*

After the initiates respond, the congregation is asked questions on the same matters: initiation, confirmation, and inclusion in the adult congregation.

- Will you, with God's help, pass to these persons the rights and responsibilities of adulthood in a way that neither overwhelms them at their young age nor denies them the opportunity for maturing further?
- Will you, with God's help, reaffirm your faith in Jesus Christ as our Lord and Savior?
- Will you, with God's help, accept them as adult members of this congregation and change your relationship of care from that of parent and child to that of adult and adult?

5. *The Commissioning*

With due solemnity the candidates kneel. Members of the congregation are invited forward to lay their hands on the heads of the initiates, transmitting authority from one generation to the next. The clergy move from person to person, placing a cross around their necks, and pronouncing a special blessing upon the newborn adult. The blessings grow out of our two years of intense living. We hope to speak to the essence of the person, summoning that unique being to become all that he or she can become.

One such blessing—to a young man who was not using his

potential and continually damned himself for this inadequacy and for making serious mistakes with his life—went as follows:

Thomas John,
You're a good man, Thomas. A very good man. Even more, you have the potential to be a great man. You have intelligence, energy, humor, good looks, perceptivity. In living life, you—like the rest of us—will have setbacks, times when hard lessons are taught. It is important that you learn those hard lessons without being hard on yourself. Remember that you are a good man, a very good man, with the potential to become a great man. So, Thomas go out into the world in peace; have courage; support the weak; honor all persons, *including yourself;* love and serve the Lord, rejoicing in the power of the Holy Spirit.

To a young woman who feared she might be cut from the same pattern as an older sister who had severe legal and psychological problems:

Emily Joan,
There will never be another one like you, Emily. You're unique . . . and uniquely gifted. Do not be embarrassed by your gifts. Use them. Share them. Give them to the lonely, the broken-hearted, those less gifted than you. And may God give you peace.

And to the woman who had nearly died in the car accident, and whose confession of faith spoke to us all with such simple eloquence:

Joy Ellen,
You know more about life and death at your young age than most of us will ever know. You have a depth that most of us will never have. Out of your depths grows a flower of a person that is good and loving and lovable. Nurture the flower of your life. Let it bloom season after season in ever more glorious ways. And remember what you taught us so well. "God has done wonderful things for us in the past. God will do the same for us in the future."

6. *Owning the Covenant*

When the commissioning is completed, the congregation officially welcomes the initiates into the body by owning the covenant that has bound together this congregation since 1668.

> We doe in ye presence of God, the Holy Angells and this Assembly, take acknowledge and Avouch the one and onely tru God, God the Father, Sone and Holy Ghost to bee our God, giving up ourselves and our children to him to be his people. Ingageing that we will walk with this God and one with another according to the rules of ye Gospell, and that we will bee subject to ye Government of Christ and observe all those Lawes yt he hath established in his Kingdome, soe far as hitherto he hath or hereafter shall be pleased to reveale ye same unto us. All this we promise lawfully to perform through the grace and strength of Christ. Grace.

7. *The Last Supper*

The newly confirmed are fully incorporated back into society when they return to the pews—*not* with their parents—and share a meal. This time, bread and wine serve as the nourishment for their new life, which stretches out into the great unknown and promises that there will be more passages, more times of crisis with attendant opportunity and danger. But they have moved through the passage to adulthood. They have negotiated much of the tricky terrain of adolescence. They have learned the techniques and mysteries that allow them to enter the first stages of their adult life with greater security and confidence than most young people have. They are ready for the rights and responsibilities of Christian maturity. They have experienced their lost rite.

Epilogue

It is almost over now. I feel as though I have been a responsible steward of the gifts given by God. The vision has been lived four times, and written once. It has been a joy. It also has been exhausting. I'm ready to lie down and rest.

There are just two short miles to go before I sleep—two promises to keep:

The first promise is to acknowledge the wonderful support given to me by so many people. Closest to me is my wife, Melissa, who has been most gracious in giving me time and space to dream dreams and to live visions—and even to write reports of how those visions came to life. She has given me invaluable feedback on both my writing and my living. My dear friend Steve Bank has encouraged me by his great capacity to honor me. Several persons have given hours and hours of work at various typewriters—John Myers, Cele Muller, and Joanne Thompson. Competent and caring persons, they gave me much more than clean copy. Two persons have edited the manuscript in truly loving ways—Kay Butterfield of First Church and Bob Koenig of The Pilgrim Press. Four clergy persons have shared the task of leading initiations with me—Gary Smith, Bonnie Rosborough, Jennie Browne, and Talitha Arnold. Innumerable persons in the congregation of First Church and the community of Middletown have given time and energy in supporting this effort. Finally, nearly one hundred adolescents have covenanted with one another and with me to walk the path to adulthood. They have allowed me to tell the story of their journey. To all, I am deeply grateful.

The second promise is one that I made to myself again and again as I read books about programs in churches. I promised to describe the relationship between our program and this book.

I hope the book is of value. I know the program is. I also know that in many ways the book is better than the program. But in some ways, the program is better than the book.

Let me explain. The book makes the program sound more unified, more carefully conceived, more orderly than it actually is. The book is neat. It has been edited and revised so that it makes more sense than ever could come in the chaotic world of adolescence. For any deception, I apologize.

Yet, that is only half the story. In many ways, the program is better than the book. I have honored my vow to keep confidences—and therefore have not told all. More important, there is no way that I can capture in words an experience that has been lived so intensely for two years. That experience can be recaptured only as one enters the arena of adolescence, armed with some of the ideas from this book, wrestling the demons, and experiencing the dynamics of the age.

That, I guess, is the purpose of this book. Whether the book is better than the program, or vice versa, makes little difference. One empowers the other. That of value in one strengthens the other.

And if anything in this book gives birth to new possibilities in your life, then surely the book has been of value.

Notes

Prologue

1. Norman O. Brown, *Love's Body* (Random House, Inc., New York, 1966), p. 15.

2. Joseph Campbell, *Hero with a Thousand Faces* (Princeton University Press, Princeton, N.J., 1949), p. 104.

Chapter One: Passages and Their Rites

1. Victor Turner, "Passages, Margins, and Poverty: Religious Symbols of Communitas", *Worship* (Vol. 46, August, 1972), p. 400.

2. Arnold van Gennep, *Rites of Passage,* translated by Monika B. Visedom and Gabrielle L. Chaffee (University of Chicago Press, Chicago, 1960), p. vii

3. Van Gennep, p. 21.

4. Van Gennep, p vii.

5. Mircea Eliade, *Rites and Symbols of Initiation: Mysteries of Birth and Rebirth.* (Harper Torch Books, New York, 1965), p. xii.

6. Alan R. Tippett, "Initiation Rites and Functional Substitutes", *Practical Anthropology* (Vol. 10, April, 1963), p. 68.

7. Tippett, p. 67.

Chapter Two: Initiation Rites

1. Joseph Campbell, *Hero With a Thousand Faces* (Princeton University Press, Princeton, N.J., 1949), p. 100

2. Joseph Henderson, *Thresholds of Initiation,* (Wesleyan University Press, Middletown, Conn., 1967), p. 53.

3. Bruno Bettelheim, *Symbolic Wounds: Puberty Rites*

and the Envious Male (Collier Books, New York, 1954), pp. 133-4. This ritual comes from the Ceray people of the Indonesian Islands.

4. Eliade, p. 26.

5. James W. Douglas, *Resistance and Contemplation: The Way of Liberation* (Dell, New York, 1972) p. 145.

6. Margaret Mead, *From the South Seas: Studies of Adolescence and Sex in Primitive Societies* (William Morrow & Co., New York, 1939), p. 73.

7. Eliade, pp. ix-x.

8. This section on initiation rites in higher religions relies heavily on material in Christine Price, *Happy Days* (United States Committee for UNICEF, United Nations, 1969), pp 88f.

9. Theodor H. Gaster, *The Holy and the Profane: Evolution of Jewish Folkways* (William Sloane Assoc., New York, 1955), p. 70 as quoted in Jack D. Spiro, "Educational Significance of the Bar Mitzphah Celebration," *Religious Education* (Vol. 72, July-August, 1977) p. 397.

Chapter Three: Scriptural Models of Initiation

1. Theodor Reik, *Mystery on the Mountain: The Drama of the Sinai Revelation* (Harper & Brothers, New York, 1959), p. 71.

2. This understanding of the Sinai experience is derived from Theodor Reik in *Mystery on the Mountain;* see especially p. 87.

3. "Bar Mitzvah", *Encyclopedia of Jewish Thought,* R. J. Zwiwerblosky and Geoffrey Wigoder, General Eds. (Holt, Rinehart and Winston, Inc., New York, 1965) p. 57.

4. All four gospels give accounts of the Last Supper. The most elaborate statement is found in the Gospel of John, Chapters 13-17.

Chapter Four: Initiation in the Christian Tradition

1. Joseph F. Kett, *Rites of Passage: Adolescence in*

America, 1790 to the Present (Basic Books, New York, 1977), p. 80.

2. Reprinted in Kett, p. 209.

3. William S. Heywood, ed., *Autobiography of Adin Ballou: 1803-1890* (Princeton University Press, Princeton, N.J., 1968), p. 106.

4. Robert E. Koenig, "Confirmation," *Church School Worker* (September 1967), p. 22.

5. Koenig, (October, 1967) p. 19.

6. "Confirmation/Youth, 1976": Research Report of the Board of Homeland Ministries, United Church of Christ.

7. Koenig (September, 1967), p. 21.

8. Aidan Kavanagh, *The Shape of Baptism: The Rite of Christian Initiation* (Pueblo Publishing Company, New York, 1978), p. xi.

9. Kavanagh, p. xiv.

10. Kavanagh, pp. 28-9.

11. Kavanagh, p. 9.

12. "The Teaching of the Twelve Apostles, Commonly Called the Didache," *Early Christian Fathers,* edited by Cyril C. Richardson, Westminster Press, Philadelphia, 1953, p. 174.

13. Grove Liturgical Study, No. 8, *Hippolytus: A Text for Students,* translated and edited by Geoffrey J. Cuming, copyright 1976 by Geoffrey J. Cuming. Reprinted by permission of the publisher, Grove Books, Bramcote, Nottingham, Great Britain.

14. Hippolytus, p. 15.

15. Hippolytus, p. 16.

16. Hippolytus, p. 16.

17. Hippolytus, p. 17.

18. Hippolytus, p. 17.

19. Hippolytus, pp. 18-20.

20. Quoted in Nathan Mitchell, "Christian Initiation: Decline and Dismemberment," *Worship* (Vol. 48, October 1974), p. 473.

21. Kavanagh, p. 69.

22. Calvin's Tracts and Treatises, translated by Henry Beveridge, edited by Thomas F. Torrance, (Oliver and Boyd, Ltd., Edinburgh, 1958), Vol. III, p. 275. Quoted in Dale Moody, *Baptism: Foundation for Christian Unity* (Westminster Press, Philadelphia, 1967), p. 48.

23. John Calvin, *Institutes of the Christian Religion,* translated by Ford Lewis Battles, edited by John T. McNeill (Westminster Press, 1960), Book IV, Chapter XV, #1, pp. 1303-4.

24. Calvin, IV, XVI, #20, p. 1342.

25. Quoted in Moody, p. 55.

26. Karl Barth, *The Teaching of the Church Regarding Baptism,* translated by E.A. Payne (SCM Press, Ltd., London, 1948), p. 14, quoted by Moody, p. 59.

27. Barth, p. 55, quoted in Moody, p. 63.

28. Barth, p. 40, quoted in Moody, p. 62.

29. Aidan Kavanagh, "Unfinished and Unbegun Revisited: The Rite of Christian Initiation of Adults," *Worship* (Vol. 53, January 1979), p. 327.

30. Louis Weil, *Christian Initiation: A Theological and Pastoral Commentary on the Proposed Rites* (Associated Parishes, Inc., Alexandria, Va., undated), p. 1.

31. Weil, p. 3

32. Weil, p. 6.

33. Weil, p. 14.

34. Frank T. Fair, *Orita for Black Youth* (Judson Press, Valley Forge, Pa., 1977), pp. 7-8.

35. Michael Dujarier, "Developments in Christian Initiation in West Africa," *Structures of Initiation in Crisis,* edited by Luis Maldonado and David Power. (Seabury Press, N.Y.), p. 59.

36. Dujarier, p. 60.

37. F. W. Dillistone, *Christianity and Symbolism* (Westminster Press, Philadelphia, 1955), p. 187.

38. Kavanagh, *Shape,* p. 115.

39. Mitchell, p. 479.

40. Quoted in Mitchell, p. 462.

41. Hippolytus, p. 18.

42. Calvin, IV, XVI, #20, p. 1343.

43. Kavanagh, *Shape,* p. 108.

44. Kavanagh, *Shape,* p. 109.

Chapter Five: The Wilderness of Adolescence

1. Irene M. Joselyn, *Adolescence* (Harper & Row, New York, 1971), pp. 9-10.

2. Edgar Friedenberg, *The Vanishing Adolescent* (Dell, New York, 1963), p. 17.

3. David Elkind "Why Children Need Time," *Parade,* (Jan. 10, 1982), p. 16.

4. Abel Pasquier, "Initiation and Society," *Structures of Initiation in Crisis,* p. 10.

5. Kett, p. 265.

6. Peter Blos, *On Adolescence: A Psychoanalytic Interpretation* (The Free Press, New York, 1965), p. 11.

7. Blos, p. 11.

8. Joselyn, pp. 32, 311.

9. Kett, p. 127.

10. Eric Erickson, "Youth: Fidelity and Identity," in *Youth: Challenge and Change* (Basic Books, Inc., New York, 1963) p. 11.

Chapter Six: A Congregation Moves into the Wilderness

1. Paul Tournier, *Secrets,* translated by Joe Embry (John Knox Press, Richmond, Va., 1963), p. 31.

2. Sigmund Freud, "Analysis of a Case of Hysteria," *Collected Papers* (Basic Books, New York, 1959), III, pp. 131-2 as quoted in Rollo May, *Love and Will* (W. W. Norton, New York, 1969), p. 144.

3. Erickson, *Youth,* p. 21.

Chapter Seven: A Way Through The Wilderness

1. John H. Westeroff, III, *Will Our Children Have Faith?* (Seabury, New York, 1976), pp. 66-7.

2. *Plea Bargaining: A Game of Criminal Justice* (La Jolla, CA: Simile II, 1971), *Baldicer* (Atlanta: John Knox Press, 1970). *Humanus* (LaJolla, CA: Simile II, 1976), *Starpower* (La Jolla, CA: Simile II, 1970).

3. Erickson, "Youth," p. 11.

4. Kenneth Kenniston, "Social Change in America," in *Youth: Challenge and Change,* p. 178.

5. Kett, p. 105.

6. James Michael Lee, ed., *The Religious Education We Need* (Religious Education Press, Inc., Mishawaka, Ind., 1977), p. 186.

7. Brown, pp. 96-7.

8. Ronald L. Grimes, "Masking: Toward a Phenomenology of Exteriorization," *Journal of American Academy of Religion,* Vol. LIII (Sept., 1975), pp. 510-12.

9. The Unitarian-Universalist Church has developed an excellent program on sexuality. We have benefited from their lists of vocabulary words and questions.

10. Quoted in William Kip, *The History, Object, and Proper Observance of the Holy Season of Lent,* (Albany, NY: E. H. Pease, 1844), pp. 20-21).

11. "Christian, Dost Thou See Them." *Pilgrim Hymnal,* (Pilgrim Press, Boston, 1958), #364.

12. Our primary reference for this unit on spirituality is *Confirming Our Faith.* (United Church Press, New York, 1980).

13. Theodore C. Braun, quoted in Loring D. Chase, *Words of Faith* (United Church Press, Boston, 1968), p. 1.

14. Kavanagh, *Shape,* p. 109.

15. Kavanagh, *Shape,* p. 108.